YUKICHI FUKUZAWA

AND THE MAKING OF THE MODERN WORLD

by Alan Macfarlane

TABLE OF CONTENTS

Preface and acknowledgements	3
Short Titles of Works by Fukuzawa (1835-1901)	5
1 Who was Fukuzawa and why is he important?	6
2 Early Life and Experiences	9
3 Character and Personality	18
4 Travels in Japan, America and Europe	26
5 The Comparative Thinker	34
6 The Making of a New Japan	39
7 Combining Western Science and Eastern Spirit	47
8 Methods in the Study of Civilization	54
9 The Civilizing Process	59
10 The Separation of Spheres	62
11 Liberty and Equality	67
12 Family Relations	71
13 The Achievement and the Legacy	82
Bibliography	85
Appendix: Fukuzawa on Family and Civilization	86

Preface and acknowledgements

My book *The Making of the Modern World; Visions from the West and East* was published by Palgrave in 2002. It discussed the work of two major writers who had dedicated their lives to trying to answer the riddle of how our modern world originated and what its future might be. These were F.W.Maitland and Yukichi Fukuzawa.

The book was only modestly successful and never went into paperback. By combining these thinkers, the distinctive contribution of each one may have been somewhat muffled. This long and expensive book did not reach a wider audience who might be potentially interested in one or other of the authors treated, but not both of them at once.

So I have decided to re-issue each part as a downloadable electronic book. This book on Fukuzawa was originally published in a section of five chapters, which have now been broken down into smaller chapters.

Apart from correcting a few minor errors I have not otherwise altered the text. Since I wrote the original chapters some ten years ago, there has been further work on the problems which Fukuzawa addressed. To have incorporated this more recent work would have created a different book, especially as my own ideas on Fukuzawa have been changing. I hope one day to consider this new work in a wider appraisal of not only Fukuzawa but of my whole attempt to pursue the 'riddle of the world'.

*

As with all books, this is a composite work and I would like to thank some of the many people who have helped me on the way to completing it. Andrew Morgan originally inspired me with a love of history and much later read through the text several times. Iris Macfarlane read the text several times. John Davey read the original typescript twice and was his usual encouraging and wise self. Cecilia Scurrah Ehrhart carefully checked the footnotes. Lily Blakely through her birth gave me inspiration.

To these I would like to add the University of Tokyo, and in particular Professor Takeo Funabiki, which funded a sabbatical term during which, among other things, I re-wrote sections of the text. Marilyn Strathern for, once again, shielding me from administrative pressures and for wise leadership. To Cherry Bryant for reading and checking the text several times. I would like also to thank Dai Toizumi, who read the whole book twice and gave helpful advice.

I originally became interested in Fukuzawa in 1990 when I visited Japan for the first time at the invitation of Professor Kenichi Nakamura of Hokkaido University. He arranged for a British Council Visiting Scholarship and was my host. His wife, Professor Toshiko Nakamura, introduced me to Fukuzawa on whom she had been working for some years. This book is in many ways the culmination of a joint project with her and I am particularly delighted to include an appendix on some of her latest findings at the end. Without her guidance, and the friendship over the years with the Nakamuras, this book could not have been written. A fuller acknowledgement and description of our collaborative work is contained in the preface to my recent book *Japan Through the Looking Glass* (2007). A number of other scholars in Japan, also acknowledged more fully in that preface, have greatly enriched my knowledge of Japanese history and philosophy.

The late Gerry Martin was over the years a constant source of support and inspiration. He read the whole text several times and we discussed it at length. In many ways this is a collaborative work with him also, and I owe him a great deal for his many kindnesses. Also I thank Hilda Martin for her friendship, encouragement and support. Finally, Sarah Harrison has, as always, given enormous help in every possible way, including several constructive readings of the text which helped to shorten it by a quarter. This book is likewise a collaborative work with her.

Short titles of works by Fukuzawa (1835-1901)

'Kyuhanjo': *Kyuhanjo* [Early Life], tr. Carmen Blacker, *Monumenta Nipponica*, IX, no. 1/2, Tokyo, 1953

Civilization: *An Outline of a Theory of Civilization*, tr. David A.Dilworth & G.Cameron Hurst, Tokyo, 1973

Learning: *An Encouragement of Learning*, tr. David A.Dilworth & Umeyo Hirano, Tokyo, 1969

Autobiography: *The Autobiography of Yukichi Fukuzawa*, tr. by Eiichi Kiyooka, New York, 1972

Speeches: *The Speeches of Fukuzawa*, tr. & ed. Wayne H. Oxford, Tokyo, 1973

Women: *Fukuzawa Yukichi on Japanese Women*, ed. Eiichi Kiyooka, Tokyo, 1988

Collected Works: *The Collected Works of Fukuzawa*, tr. Eiichi Kiyooka, Tokyo, 1980

1. WHO WAS FUKUZAWA AND WHY IS HE IMPORTANT?

Yukichi Fukuzawa (1835-1901) is arguably the greatest Japanese social thinker of the last three centuries, yet he is little known outside his native country, except to experts on Japan. Contemporaries, on the other hand, recognized his eminence and influence.

The American zoologist Edward Morse wrote that 'I received an invitation to lecture before Mr. Fukuzawa's famous school. Among the many distinguished men I have met in Japan, Mr. Fukuzawa impressed me as one of the sturdiest in activity and intellect.'[1] William Griffis, another perceptive visitor, described him as 'A student first of Dutch in the early fifties, and one of the first to cross oceans and see America and Europe, he wrote a book on the 'Manners and Customs in the Western World', which was eagerly read by millions of his hermit countrymen and served powerfully to sway Japan in the path of Western civilization.'[2] Griffis 'knew Fukuzawa well, and was, with him, a member of the Mei-Roku Sha, a club which, as its name imports, was founded in the sixth year of Meiji (1873).'[3] He described how 'As a pioneer and champion of Western civilization, and the writer of books which had reached the total sale of four million copies, he was described by the natives as 'the greatest motive force of Japanese civilization,' and by Professor Chamberlain as 'the intellectual father of half the young men who fill the middle and lower posts in the government of Japan.'"[4]

As Basil Hall Chamberlain wrote, 'In our own day, a new light arose in the person of Fukuzawa Yukichi, the 'Sage of Mita' thus called from the district of Tokyo in which he latterly resided. So wide-spread is the influence exercised by this remarkable man that no account of Japan, however brief, would be complete without some reference to his life and opinions.'[5] He likened him to Benjamin Franklin and noted that 'Like the French encyclopaedists, he laboured for universal enlightenment and social reform.'[6] At about the same time Alice Bacon wrote that 'In the whole list of publications on the woman question, nothing has ever come out in Japan that compares for outspokenness and radical sentiments with a book published within a year or two by Mr. Fukuzawa, the most influential teacher that Japan has seen in this era of enlightenment.'[7]

As a recent historian has written, 'Whereas other Japanese became caught up in the small facets of Western civilization, Fukuzawa sought to integrate these facets and observe the overall organization that made this civilization function...In short, he tried to grasp not only the technology but also the social aspects of Western civilization.'[8] His published works fill many volumes and

---

[1] Morse, **Day**, ii, 205; Edward Morse was one of the most acute and intelligent of the foreign visitors to Japan during the Meiji period.
[2] Griffis, **Mikado**, ii, 660
[3] Griffis, **Mikado**, ii, 661
[4] Griffis, **Mikado**, ii, 660
[5] Chamberlain, **Things**, 365
[6] Chamberlain, **Things**, 366-7
[7] Bacon, **Japanese Girls**, 307
[8] Hirakawa Sukehiro in Jansen (ed.), **Cambridge**, v, 460-1

'cover a variety of subjects ranging from philosophy to women's rights.'[1] As well as this he founded Keio University, a national newspaper and introduced the art of public speaking and debate in Japan.

Of course he is not the only important Japanese thinker, writer and reformer during the second half of the nineteenth century. Blacker has described some of the other 'Japanese Enlightenment' thinkers with whom he worked and argued.[2] Beasley has surveyed some of the other well-known Japanese who went on voyages to America and England and brought back information about the west.[3] Sukehiro presents a general account of a whole set of reformers and thinkers working to understand how Japan and the West could be integrated.[4] In the next generation there were notable writers and thinkers such as Mori Ogai.[5] A sense of the lively debates, in which Fukuzawa was the most famous and distinguished, but only one among many, is given by the 'Journal of the Japanese Enlightenment', **Meiroku Zasshi**, the first 43 issues of which (1874-5) have been published and which discuss many of the topics to which Fukuzawa addressed himself.[6] Like all great thinkers, it is false to isolate Fukuzawa. He was part of a network. Yet by general consent he is the greatest of them all and as long as we bear in mind that many of his ideas were matters of widespread discussion and excitement, it seems reasonable to focus on his work. If we do so we can learn a great deal.

Fukuzawa pursued Bacon's **New Atlantis**, encouraging learning, debate, controversy and investigation. His influence was immense and we can now read his work as a revealing mirror of capitalist civilization as it penetrated into Eastern Asia and was reflected back by a part of the world which has now taken many of its lessons to heart. When he died in 1901 his funeral reflected the austerity and dedication of his life. The **Japan Weekly Mail** wrote that 'No style of funeral could have been better suited to the unostentatious simplicity that marked the life of the great philosopher.'[7] His greatest successor, Maruyama Masao, in the black days of 1943, began an essay on him "Fukuzawa Yukichi was a Meiji thinker, but at the same time he is a thinker of the present day."[8] Like Montesquieu, Smith and Tocqueville he has become immortal.

The dialogue with Fukuzawa has a somewhat different purpose from that with earlier thinkers of the western Enlightenment treated in my previous work. The work of Montesquieu, Smith and Tocqueville, when combined, set out a set of conjectures as to how mankind could and perhaps did 'escape' from the normal tendencies of agrarian civilization. Since Fukuzawa (1835-1901) was writing later, and at a great distance from the original 'escape', it is unlikely that he will be able to contribute much that is original to the analysis of this problem. For that we have already considered Maitland's impressive solution. On the other hand, Fukuzawa provides an interesting test case for the utility of their theories.

---

[1] Kodansha, **Illustrated Encyclopedia**, 429
[2] Blacker, **Fukuzawa**, esp. ch.4 on 'The New Learning'
[3] Beasley, **Japan**, esp. chs. 4 and 5.
[4] Sukehiro in Jansen (ed.), **History of Japan**, ch.7
[5] See for example Bowring, **Ogai**.
[6] Braisted (trans.), **Meiroku Zasshi**
[7] Quoted in Blacker, **Fukuzawa**, 13
[8] Quoted in Craig, 148

If their model is plausible and seems to have explanatory power, it should be attractive to a thinker whose aim, as we shall see, is to grasp the essence of the first transition from agrarian to industrial civilization so that he can help his own Japanese civilization achieve a similar break-through. If he selects and approves the same central essence as Montesquieu, Smith, Tocqueville and Maitland, their insights would appear to have cross-cultural validity.

An even more stringent test is the degree of success in the material world. In other words, did the recipe work? If an outsider to Europe not only repeated the central theories of those who addressed the riddle of the origins of the modern world, but then applied these to a distant civilization and helped to effect a similar 'escape' in entirely different circumstances, this would be as good a confirmation of the validity of the theory as one could hope for.

The task is made more worthwhile because, despite his eminence and interest, there has only been one book about him in English, and that was also about other thinkers in the Japanese Enlightenment.[1] There have been one or two articles also, but there is no recent intellectual biography of a man who had an enormous impact on Japanese civilization and whose ideas are such a wonderful mirror of western thought and colonial expansion.

---

[1] Blacker, **Fukuzawa**

2. EARLY LIFE AND EXPERIENCE

Fukuzawa was born in January 1835 in Osaka, in the same year that Tocqueville's **Democracy in America** (volume one) was published. He wrote that, 'My father, Fukuzawa Hyakusuke, was a samurai belonging to the Okudaira Clan of Nakatsu on the island of Kyushu. My mother, called O-Jun as her given name, was the eldest daughter of Hashimoto Hamaemon, another samurai of the same clan.'[1] One of the shaping events of his life occurred when 'A year and a half later, in June, my father died. At that time, my brother was only eleven, and I was a mere infant, so the only course for our mother to follow was to take her children back with her to her original feudal province of Nakatsu, which she did.'[2] Thus Fukuzawa 'never knew my own father and there is preserved no likeness of his features.'[3] All that he really seems to have known of him was that he was a scholarly man and that he was unusually sympathetic to those of an inferior rank to himself. Both were characteristics which Fukuzawa tried to live up to.

The scholarly and educational side of his father's interests and then his sudden death at the age of forty-four had a double effect. On the one hand he was aware of his 'father's large collection of books...There were over fifteen hundred volumes in the collection, among them some very rare ones. For instance, there were Chinese law books of the Ming dynasty...'[4] He heard that his father had expressed an interest in his becoming trained to be a monk and this seems to have given Fukuzawa impetus to study.[5] On the other hand the normal Chinese, neo-Confucian education which he would have been subjected to, in all probability, if his father had lived was denied him. 'There were no funds to send him to school until he was 14, almost ten years after the usual age for starting school.'[6] Fukuzawa himself noted one of the consequences. 'First of all, I lacked someone to look after my education and I grew up without learning calligraphy very well. I might have studied it later in life, but then I had already gone into Western sciences, and was regarding all Chinese culture as a mortal enemy.'[7] He lamented the loss of the artistic skill. 'This peculiar whim of mine was a great mistake. Indeed, my father and my brother were both cultured men. Especially my brother was a fine calligrapher, and something of a painter and sealcutter, too. But I fear I have none of those qualities. When it comes to antiques, curios, and other branches of the fine arts, I am hopelessly out of it.'[8] Yet it is perhaps not too speculative to suggest that it was the absence of a formal education of the old style which partly set him on an original course for life.

When Fukuzawa's mother moved back from Osaka to the remote Kyushu domain of her husband's clan she kept the memory of her dead husband alive, in particular because of her isolation with her children.

---

[1] Fukuzawa, **Autobiography**, 1
[2] Fukuzawa, **Autobiography**, 12
[3] Fukuzawa, **Autobiography**, 303
[4] Fukuzawa, **Autobiography**, 44
[5] Fukuzawa, **Autobiography**, 5-6
[6] Nishikawa, 'Fukuzawa',3
[7] Fukuzawa, **Autobiography**, 296
[8] Fukuzawa, **Autobiography**, 296

> My father's ideas survived him in his family. All five of us children lived with few friends to visit us, and since we had no one to influence us but our mother who lived only in her memory of her husband, it was as if father himself were living with us. So in Nakatsu, with our strange habits and apparel, we unconsciously formed a group apart, and although we never revealed it in words, we looked upon the neighbours around us as less refined than ourselves.[1]

The isolation and independence of the returned family with their city ways and costumes early created several key features of Fukuzawa's personality and is perceptively described by him as follows.

> Moreover, my mother, although she was a native of Nakatsu, had accustomed herself to the life of Osaka, then the most prosperous city in Japan, and so the way she dressed us and arranged our hair made us seem queer in the eyes of these people in a secluded town on the coast of Kyushu. And having nothing else to wear but what we had brought from Osaka, we naturally felt more comfortable to stay at home and play among ourselves.[2]

The effects of isolation gave Fukuzawa's mother especial power and it is clear that not only was she an out of the ordinary woman, but that many of Fukuzawa's central interests in life, including the position of women in society, stemmed from her personality and attitudes. He described how 'My mother was an unusual woman who thought individually on certain matters. In religion she did not seem to have a belief like that of other old women of the time. Her family belonged to the Shin sect of Buddhism, yet she would never go to hear a sermon as was expected of everyone in that sect.'[3] Equally important was her egalitarian attitude, a continuation of that of her late husband.

> My mother was fond of doing kindnesses to all people, especially of making friends among the classes beneath her own, the merchants and farmers. She had no objection even to admitting beggars, or even the outcast **eta** (the slaughterers of cattle and dealers in leather who were a separate class by themselves). My mother never showed any sign of slighting them and her way of speaking to them was very respectful. Here is an instance of my mother's charity, which I remember with both affection and distaste.[4]

Fukuzawa claimed that he early learnt to treat those who were theoretically inferior with respect. 'So I believe my feeling of respect for all people was bred in me by the custom of my parents. In Nakatsu I never made a show of my rank in my mingling with any persons, even with the merchants of the town or the farmers outside.'[5] Thus he lived as a happy, but somewhat isolated little boy, playing with his four siblings but cut off from others. 'I still remember that I was always a lively happy child, fond of talk and romping about, but I was never good at climbing trees and I never learned to swim. This was perhaps because I did not play with the neighbourhood children.'[6]

Life in the clan.

Much of Fukuzawa's work can only be understood when we realize the clan background into which he moved, and from which he sought to escape. The

---

[1] Fukuzawa, **Autobiography**, 3
[2] Fukuzawa, **Autobiography**, 2
[3] Fukuzawa, **Autobiography**, 14
[4] Fukuzawa, **Autobiography**, 15
[5] Fukuzawa, **Autobiography**, 180
[6] Fukuzawa, **Autobiography**, 4

world of rigid social hierarchy which he so vividly describes, and which provided the shock of contrast with the West and the emerging new world of Japan after the Meiji Restoration of 1868, fixed him initially as a member of an **Ancien Regime**. It was an hierarchical civilization which he partially rejected and which crumbled away around him in a revolution as dramatic, if less bloody, than that through which France went after 1789.

In his work on **Civilization** Fukuzawa gave a brief autobiographical account of the world of his youth.

> I was born into a family of minor retainers in the service of a weak **fudai** [hereditary house] daimyo during the time of the Tokugawa shogunate. When within the **han** [domain] I met some illustrious high retainer or samurai, I was always treated with contempt; even as a child I could not help but feel resentment... Again, when I travelled outside the **han** confines I would run into Court nobles, officials of the Bakufu, or retainers of the three branch families of the Tokugawa house. At post towns they would monopolize the palanquins, at river crossings they would be ferried over first; since high and low were not permitted to stay at the same time in the same lodging house, there were times when I was suddenly turned out in the middle of the night.[1]

Now, writing in the 1870's, 'the circumstances of those days seem ridiculous', but 'it is still possible to imagine the rage felt at the time those things happened.'[2] In a fascinating autobiographical article he fills in some of the details of those early status-dominated days.

He first described the structure of his clan.

> The samurai of the old Okudaira clan of Nakatsu, from the Chief Minister down to the very lowest of those who were permitted to wear a sword, numbered about 1500 persons. They were divided broadly into two classes, though in all there were as many as a hundred different minute distinctions between their social positions and official duties. The upper of the two broad classes comprised all samurai from the Chief Minister down to the Confucian scholars, physicians and the members of the **koshogumi**, while the lower class included all those from the calligraphers, **nakakosho**, **tomokosho** and **koyakunin**, down to the **ashigaru** [foot soldier]. The upper class was about one third the size of the lower.[3]

Fukuzawa's father was a member of the lower two-thirds and a 'lower samurai, whatever his merit or talents, could never rise above an upper samurai.'[4] Thus, 'A lower samurai might therefore aspire to promotion within his own class, but he would no more hope to enter the ranks of the upper samurai than would a four-legged beast hope to fly like a bird.'[5] There was an absolute bar between lower and upper and a rule forbidding marriage. 'Under no circumstances was marriage permitted between those of the rank of **kyunin** and those of the rank of **kachi**. Such alliances were forbidden both by clan law and by custom. Even in

---

[1] Fukuzawa, **Civilization**, 185
[2] Fukuzawa, **Civilization**, 185
[3] **koshogumi** were daimyo attendants, consisting especially of boys who had not yet come of age; **nakakosho**, 'often acted as grooms and stablemen, though their studies were not necessarily fixed'; **tomokosho** 'often acted as close attendants on the daimyo, walking behind him carrying his sword' etc.; **koyakunin** were 'low ranking samurai with various light duties such as guarding the gate'; **ashigaru** were the 'lowest rank of samurai, sometimes hardly considered to have samurai status', Fukuzawa, **Kyuhanjo**, 309
[4] Fukuzawa, **Kyuhanjo**, 309
[5] Fukuzawa, **Kyuhanjo**, 310

cases of adultery, both parties nearly always came from the same class. It was extremely rare to find men and women from different classes forming illicit unions.'¹

The status difference between upper and lower samurai was fixed by birth and marriage and affected every aspect of life. The lowest rank of lower samurai, the **ashigaru**, 'always had to prostrate himself on the ground in the presence of an upper samurai. If he should encounter an upper samurai on the road in the rain, he had to take off his **geta** [shoes] and prostrate himself by the roadside.'² 'Upper samurai rode on horseback; lower samurai went on foot. Upper samurai possessed the privileges of hunting wild boar and fishing; lower samurai had no such privileges. Sometimes it even happened that a lower samurai was refused formal permission to go to another province to study, on the score that learning was not considered proper to his station.'³ The upper samurai always showed their status by their dress and attendants. 'When they went out of doors they always wore **hakama** [formal trousers] and two swords, and whenever they went out at night they were always accompanied by lanterns. Some even went so far as to have lanterns on bright moonlight nights.'⁴ Written and spoken language reflected the differences. 'In letters too there were various rigid and strictly differentiated modes of address, the character **sama** being written differently according to the rank of the person to whom the letter was addressed. In spoken forms of address all upper samurai, regardless of age, addressed lower samurai as 'Kisama", while lower samurai addressed upper samurai as 'Anata'.'⁵ Indeed, 'There were innumerable other differences in speech besides these ... Thus if one heard a conversation the other side of a wall, one would know immediately if those talking were upper samurai, lower samurai, merchants or farmers.'⁶

There were many other differences; 'the upper samurai differed from the lower in rights, kinship, income, education, household economy, manners and customs. It was therefore only natural that their standards of honour and fields of interest should also differ.'⁷ There were equal differences between the lower samurai and the other orders of peasants, artisans, merchants and 'outcastes'. The feeling of sullen resentment this created, certainly in Fukuzawa's memory, is palpable. 'The spirit of the times, however, insisted on a strict observance of one's station in life and on preserving a fixed and immovable order in everything, and this spirit forbade the lower samurai to express outwardly the doubt and anger which they constantly harboured.'⁸

All of this was part of the structure which had evolved in the form of 'centralized feudalism' which had already existed for over two hundred years of unprecedented peace under the Tokugawa Shogunate by Fukuzawa's birth.

---

¹Fukuzawa, **Kyuhanjo**, 311; the use of the terms **kyunin** for upper samurai, and **kachi** for lower samurai, we are told is 'unusual, and may have been peculiar to the Nakatsu clan'.
²Fukuzawa, **Kyuhanjo**, 310
³Fukuzawa, **Kyuhanjo**, 311
⁴Fukuzawa, **Kyuhanjo**, 317
⁵Fukuzawa, **Kyuhanjo**, 310-1
⁶Fukuzawa, **Kyuhanjo**, 318
⁷Fukuzawa, **Kyuhanjo**, 318
⁸Fukuzawa, **Kyuhanjo**, 318

Officially the role of the samurai was to provide the middle level of the military and civilian bureaucracy. Hence each clan was given a corporate existence and corporate estate with a fixed rice rent of a certain amount in order to perform its functions. In theory, the samurai, upper and lower, were meant to be a military and literate elite, who kept themselves away from all mundane tasks such as business, trade, manufacturing and so on. In practice, however, for some time past, the lower samurai had been experiencing an economic crisis which made it impossible for them to avoid becoming engaged in practical activities. Fukuzawa gives a fascinating account of their predicament.

> The lower samurai ... received stipends of fifteen **koku** plus rations for three, thirteen **koku** plus rations for two, or ten **koku** plus rations for one. Some received a money stipend of even less than this. Those of middle rank and above received a net income no higher than from seven to ten **koku**. At this rate a man and his wife living alone might manage without hardship, but if there were four or five children or old people in the family, this income was not sufficient to cover even the necessities of life such as food and clothing.[1]

The situation forced the lower samurai into a calculative and entrepreneurial mode unknown by the upper strata. 'The lower samurai had to work with both income and expenditure in mind, and hence had to plan their household economy with a minuteness never dreamt of by the upper samurai.'[2]

The only solution was to abandon the principle that samurai did not work with their hands. Thus

> everyone in the family capable of work, both men and women alike, eked out a poor livelihood by odd jobs such as spinning and handicrafts. These jobs might in theory be mere sidework, but in fact the samurai came to regard them as their main occupation, relegating their official clan duties to the position of sidework. These men were therefore not true samurai. It would be more correct to say that they were a kind of workmen. Thus harassed by the task of making a mere living for themselves, they had no time in which to give a thought to their children's education. The lower samurai were thus very ill versed in literature and other high forms of learning, and not unnaturally came to have the bearing and deportment of humble workmen.[3]

Fukuzawa further described that this had been a growing tendency since

> for twenty or thirty years the sidework of the lower samurai had been steadily increasing. At first they did little more than joinery work in wood, making boxes and low tables, or twisting paper cords for binding hair. Gradually however their jobs increased in variety. Some made wooden clogs and umbrellas; some covered paper lanterns; some would do carpentry work in plain wood and then add to its quality by painting it with lacquer; some were so skilful in making doors and sliding screens that they could even vie with professional carpenters. Recently some began to combine handicrafts with commerce. They would build boats, lay in stock and ship it to Osaka, some travelling in the boats themselves.[4]

One consequence was that they had to neglect their official military and literary training. 'Many of them practised the military arts in such little time as they could spare from their sidework, but in literature they would get no further than the Four Books and the Five Classics, and, at a little more advanced stage,

---

[1] Fukuzawa, **Kyuhanjo**, 312-3; a **koku** is a measure of rice, the average annual consumption of one person.
[2] Fukuzawa, **Kyuhanjo**, 314
[3] Fukuzawa, **Kyuhanjo**, 313
[4] Fukuzawa, **Kyuhanjo**, 320

one or two books of Meng Ch'iu and the **Tso Chuan**.'[1] Another was that they had to forgo the supposed taboos on becoming involved in handling money, or carrying objects.

> Just as it was considered low and vulgar to go out and to make purchases, so it was thought shameful to carry things. Hence apart from fishing rods and the appurtenances of swordsmanship, no upper samurai ever carried anything in his hands, even the smallest **furoshiki** bundle. The lower samurai did not employ servants unless they happened to hold a good post or have a particularly large family. Few of them would go into the towns in daylight to make purchases, but at night it was quite customary for both men and women to go.[2]

Fukuzawa provides glimpses of his own upbringing in this ambivalent world and his family's struggle with relative poverty. 'Originally I was a country samurai, living on wheat meal and pumpkin soup, wearing out-grown homespun clothes.'[3] He recalled that 'Ever since early childhood, my brother and sisters and I had known all the hardships of poverty. And none of us could ever forget what struggles our mother had been obliged to make in the meagre household. Despite this constant hardship there were many instances of the quiet influence that mother's sincere spirit had upon us.'[4] In fact he came to relish the physical, not to say spartan, side of life.

> I was born in a poor family and I had to do much bodily work whether I liked it or not. This became my habit and I have been exercising my body a great deal ever since. In winter time, working out of doors constantly, I often had badly chapped hands. Sometimes they cracked open and bled. Then I would take needle and thread, and sew the edges of the opening together and apply a few drops of hot oil. This was our homely way of curing chapped skin back in Nakatsu.[5]

The absence of freedom and equality in the clan.

Much of Fukuzawa's greatest work would be devoted to examining how it would be possible to change Japan from this group-based and hierarchical society, to an individualistic and egalitarian one. In this work he relived his own experiences and used them to explain how he had himself escaped from such a world and how others could do so.

The clan had the right to take an individual and place him in another family, with another set of relatives, through the process of adoption. Of course this has happened to a certain extent to countless women through arranged marriage, but usually they remain part of their original family as well. In Japan it was much more extreme, and the adopted person severed links and took on the new family as his or her own. This happened twice to Fukuzawa and he even found that at one point 'I had legally become a son to my brother'.[6] It is indeed a wise son who knows his own father in such a situation and it is not surprising that individuals might feel subordinate to the group.

---

[1] Fukuzawa, **Kyuhanjo**, 313
[2] Fukuzawa, **Kyuhanjo**, 317; a **furoshiki** is a cloth for wrapping books or other objects.
[3] Fukuzawa, **Autobiography**, 331
[4] Fukuzawa, **Autobiography**, 261
[5] Fukuzawa, **Autobiography**, 329
[6] The arrangements were very complicated and only partly described in Fukuzawa, **Autobiography**, 42. I am grateful to Professor Nishikawa for advice on this point.

The lack of personal identity was mirrored in the naming system. In most western civilizations a person had one name at birth and kept it - though women often lost it at marriage. In Japan, a name was attached to a position, so if a person moved into another role, his name would change. One part of this is noted by Fukuzawa in relation to the absence of the notion of the individual: '...there is another point in which we can see the warriors of Japan lacked this individualistic spirit. That is the matter of names. Essentially, a man's name is something given him by his parents.'[1] If they wished to change his name, they could do so - as could the clan.

Of course, the degree of freedom depended on one's place in the clan system. Thus 'While my brother was living, I could go anywhere at any time with only his sanction, but now that I had become the head of the family with certain duties to the lord, I had to obtain a permit for going 'abroad'.'[2] Thus one had elements of that autocratic Confucian system found in China. The senior male was relatively powerful, sons, younger brothers and all women were largely without individual rights, subservient to the clan or household head.

Absence of individuality was symbolized and carried to its furthest extreme in the avoidance of the use of personal pronouns in Japanese. As Fukuzawa noted, 'Another problem which requires explanation is the fact that the personal pronouns, 'I', 'you', 'we', and 'us' appear frequently in my translation; whereas, in most cases, the corresponding words are omitted in the original text.'[3] In such a situation, individual opinions and rights, and independent thought do indeed meet a barrier.

The second general feature of Fukuzawa's early situation was the basic assumption of inequality. Fukuzawa was later to describe what he perceived to be the rigid and hierarchical social system of Tokugawa Japan, where men were born unequal. He described how 'In relations between men and women, the man has preponderance of power over the woman. In relations between parents and children the parent has preponderance of power over the child. In relations between elder and younger brother, and between young and old in general, the same principle holds good. Outside the family circle we find exactly the same thing.'[4] He described how 'Back in those childhood days, I lived under the iron-bound feudal system. Everywhere people clung to the ancient custom by which the rank of every member of a clan was inalterably fixed by his birth. So from father to son and grandson the samurai of high rank would retain their rank. In the same way those of lower rank would forever remain in their low position. Neither intelligence nor ability could prevent the scorn of their superiors.'[5]

> Thus what was to be found in the family and clan was to be found everywhere. Wherever there are social relationships there you will find this imbalance of power. Even within the government itself the imbalance can be extremely great, depending on the position

---

[1] Fukuzawa, **Civilization**, 156
[2] Fukuzawa, **Autobiography**, 49
[3] Fukuzawa, **Speeches**, 74.
[4] Blacker, **Fukuzawa**, 71
[5] Fukuzawa, **Autobiography**, 179

and grade of the officials. When we see a minor official brandishing his authority over one commoner we might think he is a very powerful person. But let this same official meet someone higher in the bureaucracy and he will be subjected to even worse oppression from his superior than he dealt out to the commoner.[1]

It was a system of innate inequalities, which afflicted every relationship. 'Now let me discuss this imbalance as it exists in reality. You will find this imbalance in all relations between man and woman, between parents and children, between brothers, and between young and old. Turn from the family circle to society, and relations there will be no different. Teacher and student, lord and retainer, rich and poor, noble and base-born, newcomers and oldtimers, main family and branch families - between all of these there exists an imbalance of power.'[2] The whole social structure seemed fixed, almost caste-like, and was transmitted over the generations: '...sons of high officials following their father in office, sons of foot-soldiers always becoming foot-soldiers, and those of the families in between having the same lot for centuries without change. For my father, there had been no hope of rising in society whatever effort he might make.'[3]

All this was, of course, bound up with the innate premise of superior and inferior in all relations built into Confucian thought. 'In China and Japan the ruler-subject relationship was considered inherent in human nature, so that the relationship between ruler and subject was conceived as analogous to the relationships between husband and wife and parent and child. The respective roles of ruler and subject were even thought of as predestined from a previous life. Even a man like Confucius was unable to free himself from this obsession.'[4] Oppression and servility were built deep into the system.

> Thus, even in the period of violent warfare between the samurai, this principle of social relationships could not be broken. At the head of one family was a general, and under him household elders; then came the knights, the foot-soldiers, and lastly the **ashigaru** and **chugen**. The duties of upper and lower were clear-cut, and equally clear were the rights that went with these duties. Every man submitted to overbearance from those above and required subservience from those below. Every man was both unreasonably oppressed and unreasonably oppressive.[5]

Fukuzawa's rejection of this premise of basic inequality, of subservience to those above and arrogance to those below, seems to have partly stemmed from his parents. He described how 'This respect for people of lower rank was not original with me. It had been handed down from both my parents.'[6] He described a specific example of their more open attitude. 'Nakamura was an able scholar, but he was the son of a dyer who had lived in Nakatsu. Therefore nobody in our clan would befriend this 'mere merchant's son'. My father, however, admired his personality and, disregarding all social precedents, took him into our house in Osaka and, having introduced him to many people, brought it about finally that Nakamura was made a household scholar in the

---

[1] Fukuzawa, **Civilization**, 136
[2] Fukuzawa, **Civilization**, 136
[3] Fukuzawa, **Autobiography**, 6
[4] Fukuzawa, **Civilization**, 39
[5] Fukuzawa, **Civilization**, 155
[6] Fukuzawa, **Autobiography**, 179

Minakuchi clan.'[1] More generally, the attitude was that 'the farmers and merchants - the ruled - were totally separated from the rulers, forming an entirely different world. Their attitudes and customs differed.'[2] All of this made Fukuzawa increasingly uncomfortable. He described how in his early days 'The thing that made me most unhappy in Nakatsu was the restriction of rank and position. Not only on official occasions, but in private intercourse, and even among children, the distinctions between high and low were clearly defined.'[3] His growing unease was brought to a head with the overthrow of the Tokugawa Shogunate in 1868 at the Meiji Restoration.

There must have been many boys in Fukuzawa's position, yet only one of them turned into a man who shaped the destiny of his country. Two principal factors were important in selecting him rather than others. One was a particularly stubborn and determined character, the other was chance. Let us look at his personality first.

---

[1] Fukuzawa, **Autobiography**, 180
[2] Fukuzawa, **Civilization**, 168
[3] Fukuzawa, **Autobiography**, 18

3. CHARACTER AND PERSONALITY

Fukuzawa's early life as a poor Samurai developed his character in various ways. Not only did he take unusual physical exercise, pounding rice and wood chopping, but he developed a keen interest in practical, do-it-yourself activities of a humble kind. He described how 'As I grew older, I began to do a greater variety of things, such as mending the wooden clogs and sandals - I mended them for all my family - and fixing broken doors and leaks in the roof.'[1] Poverty and pride combined to make him a practical and versatile workman, a Japanese Benjamin Franklin, which later stood him in great stead when he came to study western technology and science. 'When something fell in the well, I contrived some means to fish it out. When the lock of a drawer failed to open, I bent a nail in many ways, and poking into the mechanism, somehow opened it. These were my proud moments. I was good at pasting new paper on the inner doors of the house, which are called **shoji**. Every so often when the old lining of the **shoji** turned gray with dust, it had to be taken off and new white paper pasted on the frame.'[2]

He recalled that he early learnt that 'knowledge' consisted not only of reading books but of doing things - and not just sword play and the calligraphy he had missed. He wrote that 'My own particular talent seems to be in doing all kinds of humble work. While I was in Yamamoto's house, I did all kinds of work in his household. I do not recall ever saying, 'I cannot do this', or 'I don't want to do that.'[3] He loved tinkering with his hands. 'Thus ever since my childhood, besides my love of books, I have been accustomed to working with my hands. And even yet, in my old age, I find myself handling planes and chisels, and making and mending things.'[4] All this helped to remind him that it was not enough merely to learn, to understand, but vital also to put that learning to use. 'It is not necessary to reiterate here that learning does not consist only in the reading of books. The essence of learning lies rather in its practical application, without which learning is still ignorance.'[5]

Above all, he seems to have developed a huge, practical, curiosity and an openness of mind and scepticism about received wisdom which marks him out as unusual for his own time and again indicates his 'Enlightenment' status. One aspect of this can be seen in his attitude to the supernatural. He was brought up in a world where Shinto, Buddhist and folk superstitions mingled to fill the environment with prohibitions and danger, yet his mother's rationalism and his own curiosity led him to doubt whether there was really truth in them. He decided therefore to carry out some experiments. Two of these are worth recounting. In the first, when he was twelve or thirteen he accidentally stepped on a document naming his clan lord. His brother told him off, and though he apologized he felt angry and

---

[1] Fukuzawa, **Autobiography**, 9
[2] Fukuzawa, **Autobiography**, 9
[3] Fukuzawa, **Autobiography**, 35
[4] Fukuzawa, **Autobiography**, 10
[5] Fukuzawa, **Learning**, 75

Then I went on, reasoning in my childish mind that if it was so wicked to step on a man's name, it would be very much more wicked to step on a god's name; and I determined to test the truth. So I stole one of the charms, the thin paper slips, bearing sacred names, which are kept in many households for avoiding bad luck. And I deliberately trampled on it when nobody was looking. But no heavenly vengeance came. 'Very well,' I thought to myself. 'I will go a step further and try it in the worst place.' I took it to the **chozu-ba** (the privy) and put it in the filth. This time I was a little afraid, thinking I was going a little too far. But nothing happened. 'It is just as I thought!' I said to myself. 'What right did my brother have to scold me?' I felt that I had made a great discovery! But this I could not tell anybody, not even my mother or sisters.[1]

His scepticism grew until he tried a further test which put paid to all his supernatural fears.

When I grew older by a few years, I became more reckless, and decided that all the talk about divine punishment which old men use in scolding children was a lie. Then I conceived the idea of finding out what the god of Inari really was. There was an Inari shrine in the corner of my uncle's garden, as in many other households. I opened the shrine and found only a stone there. I threw it away and put in another stone which I picked up on the road. Then I went on to explore the Inari shrine of our neighbour, Shimomura. Here the token of the god was a wooden tablet. I threw it away too and waited for what might happen. When the season of the Inari festival came, many people gathered to put up flags, beat drums, and make offerings of the sacred rice-wine. During all the round of festival services I was chuckling to myself: 'There they are - worshipping my stones, the fools!' Thus from my childhood I have never had any fear of gods or Buddha. Nor have I ever had any faith in augury and magic, or in the fox and badger which, people say, have power to deceive men. I was a happy child, and my mind was never clouded by unreasonable fears.[2]

From then on he sought for explanations in this-worldly forces, and moved along the paths which Montesquieu, Smith and Tocqueville had all trod.

One major consequence of this was that he applied the method of doubt and scepticism to all things. Later he was to proclaim the ideology which has been enshrined from Francis Bacon to Karl Popper. 'Even today the reason that the great persons of the West lead people on the path to higher civilization is that their purpose is entirely to refute the once firm and irrefutable theories of the ancients, and to entertain doubts concerning practices about which common sense had never doubted before.'[3] It was the application of curiosity and methodical doubt to the world which had created modern science and technology he believed. 'If we seek the essence of Western civilization, it lies in the fact that they scrutinize whatever they experience with the five senses, in order to discover its essence and its functions. They go on to seek the causes of its functions, and anything they find beneficial they make use of, while whatever they find harmful they discard. The range of power of modern man is endless. He controls the energies in water and fire to power the steam engines by which he crosses the vast Pacific.'[4] His own childhood world had been different for 'the spirit of learning differs between East and West. The countries of the West stress the idea of experiment; we in Japan dote on the theories of Confucius and

---

[1] Fukuzawa, **Autobiography**, 16-7
[2] Fukuzawa, **Autobiography**, 17
[3] Fukuzawa, **Learning**, 94
[4] Fukuzawa, **Civilization**, 111-2

Mencius.'[1] Yet he had increasingly come to challenge that world, both at the social and the cosmological level.

There were disadvantages to his agnosticism. For instance, he found it more or less impossible to understand the obvious force and nature of religion in western civilization. Like Tocqueville, for example, he could see from his visits to America and Europe that Christianity played an enormously important part as a social glue and as a system of meaning. Indeed, like Tocqueville, he believed that whatever his own scepticism, it was necessary, perhaps essential, for religion to be encouraged, in a modest way. Summarizing his wishes for the future at the end of his life he wrote that 'I should like to encourage a religion - Buddhism or Christianity - to give peaceful influence on a large number of our people.'[2] He developed this idea more fully, while expressing forcefully his own agnosticism, when he stated that

> it goes without saying that the maintenance of peace and security in society requires a religion. For this purpose any religion will do. I lack a religious nature, and have never believed in any religion. I am thus open to the charge that I am advising others to be religious, when I am not so. Yet my conscience does not permit me to clothe myself with religion, when I have it not at heart. Of religions, there are several kinds. Buddhism, Christianity and what not. Yet, from my standpoint, there is no more difference between these than between green tea and black tea. It makes little difference whether you drink one or the other.'[3]

Basically, like Rousseau, Hume and others, he saw religion as perhaps a marginal social necessity, but often a superstitious nonsense that was used as a prop by the powerful: a very Enlightened and rationalist view. Yet the rationalism also made it difficult for him to understand some of the difference of East and West, 'But still I am not sure I have grasped the real causes of the great differences between the religions of the East and West.'[4]

His admission of bafflement as to causes, is, in fact, one of the reasons for our continuing interest in him. What we admire him for most of all, is his unflagging curiosity and open-mindedness. Considering the pressures upon him from his youth, he had an amazingly rational and independent mind. In his **Autobiography** he wrote of the 'irresistible fascination of our new knowledge.'[5] In his characteristically entitled **Encouragement of Learning** he stressed the need for doubt and questioning. He described to his audience how 'The progress of civilization lies in seeking the truth both in the area of physical facts and in the spiritual affairs of man. The reason for the West's present high level of civilization is that in every instance they proceeded from some point of doubt.'[6] His book had a heading, 'Methodic doubt and selective judgment' and explained that 'There is much that is false in the world of belief, and much that is true in the world of doubt.'[7] He cited famous, perhaps apocryphal, instances. 'Watt (1736-1819) entertained doubts concerning the properties of steam when he was experimenting with a boiling kettle. In all these cases they attained to the truth

---

[1] Fukuzawa, **Civilization**, 149
[2] Fukuzawa, **Autobiography**, 336
[3] Chamberlain, **Things**, 408
[4] Fukuzawa, **Learning**, 98
[5] Fukuzawa, **Autobiography**, 85
[6] Fukuzawa, **Learning**, 93
[7] Fukuzawa, **Learning**, 93

by following the road of doubt.'[1] All he could note was that 'In the countries of the West religion flourishes not only among monks in monasteries but also in secular society...and this attracts men's hearts and preserves virtuous ways. But in our Japan religion lacks this efficacy in society at large: it is solely a matter of sermons in temples.'[2]

What else can we learn about the character of the young man growing up in the remote province of a southern Japanese island in the early 1830s? One obvious characteristic was his loneliness and inner strength. Using the heading 'No-one is admitted to my inner thoughts', he described how

> From my early days in Nakatsu I have not been able to achieve what I might call a heart-to-heart fellowship with any of my friends, nor even with a relative. It was not that I was peculiar and people did not care to associate with me. Indeed, I was very talkative and quite congenial with both men and women. But my sociability did not go to the extent of opening myself completely to the confidence of others, or sharing with them the inner thoughts of my heart. I was never envious of anyone, never wished to become like someone else; never afraid of blame, nor anxious for praise. I was simply independent.[3]

That is not to say that he did not have friends; but he kept his own counsel. 'I am of a very sociable nature; I have numerous acquaintances, and among them I count a number of trusted friends. But even in these relations I do not forget my doctrine of preparing for the extreme - for a friend can change his mind.'[4]

The reserve, iron will and self reliance, obviously related to his samurai **bushido** ethic and the traditions of **zen** was consciously cultivated. 'One day while reading a Chinese book, I came upon these ancient words: 'Never show joy or anger in the face.' These words brought a thrill of relief as if I had learned a new philosophy of life.'[5] He became a working model of Kipling's **If**, treating the 'impostors' of praise and blame in the same way. 'Since then I have always remembered these golden words, and have trained myself to receive both applause and disparagement politely, but never to allow myself to be moved by either. As a result, I have never been truly angry in my life, nor have my hands ever touched a person in anger, nor has a man touched me in a quarrel, ever since my youth to this old age.'[6]

He always expected the worst. 'It has been a habit of mine to be prepared for the extreme in all situations; that is, to anticipate the worst possible result of any event so that I should not be confounded when the worst did come.'[7] He combined activity and acceptance of fate in a way that reminds one forcefully of Weber's puritan ethic. 'I have worked with energy, planned my life, made friends, endeavored to treat all men alike, encouraged friends in their need, and sought the cooperation of others as most men do. But believing as I do that the final outcome of all human affairs is in the hands of Heaven, whenever my endeavors failed, I refrained from imploring sympathy and resigned myself to

---

[1] Fukuzawa, **Learning**, 93
[2] Quoted in Craig, 'Fukuzawa', 134
[3] Fukuzawa, **Autobiography**, 290
[4] Fukuzawa, **Autobiography**, 325
[5] Fukuzawa, **Autobiography**, 19
[6] Fukuzawa, **Autobiography**, 19
[7] Fukuzawa, **Autobiography**, 324

necessity. In short, my basic principle is never to depend upon the whims of other people.'[1] He gave all he could to whatever activity he was engaged in, but accepted the outcome, in the end, was largely determined by forces outside his control. Speaking later of his attempts to set up the first Japanese university of Keio, he wrote 'Although I give the best of my ability to the management of the institution and put all my heart into it for its future and its improvement, yet I never forget that all my personal worries and immediate concerns are but a part of the 'games' of this 'floating world', our entire lives but an aspect of some higher consciousness.[2]

Two other features may be noticed. One was his immensely hard work, physical and intellectual. As a student, in particular, he worked prodigiously hard to learn Dutch and then English. He described how as a student 'I had been studying without regard to day or night. I would be reading all day and when night came I did not think of going to bed. When tired, I would lean over on my little desk, or stretch out on the floor resting my head on the raised alcove (**tokonoma**) of the room. I had gone through the year without ever spreading my pallet and covers and sleeping on the pillow.'[3] We shall see his prodigious energy and hard work manifested in an extraordinarily productive life.

A second feature was his desire to be independent of others. This manifested itself in his refusal to be sucked into any political job, as would have been natural. He later wrote that 'To speak very honestly, the first reason for my avoiding a government post is my dislike of the arrogance of all officials. It might be argued that they need to put on dignity in their office. But in reality they enjoy the bullying.'[4] But added to this was his desire to remain independent. 'All in all, I am determined to live independent of man or thing. I cannot think of government office while I hold this principle.'[5] He thought of himself as an independent spirit. 'As long as I remain in private life, I can watch and laugh. But joining the government would draw me into the practice of those ridiculous pretensions which I cannot allow myself to do.'[6] He saw himself as an analyst of politics, but not a politician or bureaucrat. 'All in all, my activities with politics have been that of a 'diagnostician'. I have no idea of curing the nation's 'disease' with my own hands nor have I ever thought of politics in connection with my personal interest.'[7] This was not through lack of interest, but a desire to keep at arm's length. 'Not that I am wholly uninterested in that field, for I frequently discuss the subject and have written upon it, but for the daily wear and tear of its practice I have no taste. I am like the diagnostician in the medical field who can judge a disease but cannot care for a sick man. So people are not to take my diagnosis of politics as any evidence of personal ambition.'[8]

His independence also showed itself in a terror of being financially involved, or at the mercy of others. Later in his life 'as if for the first time, I came to realize

---

[1] Fukuzawa, **Autobiography**, 286
[2] Fukuzawa, **Autobiography**, 325
[3] Fukuzawa, **Autobiography**, 79
[4] Fukuzawa, **Autobiography**, 309
[5] Fukuzawa, **Autobiography**, 315
[6] Fukuzawa, **Autobiography**, 309
[7] Fukuzawa, **Autobiography**, 321
[8] Fukuzawa, **Autobiography**, 315

that I had never borrowed any money in my life. That had always seemed natural to me, but it appears it was rather unusual in other people's eyes.'[1] At the end of his life, aged sixty-five, he noted that 'since I left home in Nakatsu at twenty-one, I have been managing my own affairs; and since my brother's death when I was twenty-three, I have assumed the care of my mother and niece. At twenty-eight I was married, had children, and took all the responsibilities of a family on myself.'[2]

Fukuzawa clearly took pleasure in 'going against the grain', however difficult it was. 'In anything, large or small, it is difficult to be the pioneer. It requires an unusual recklessness. But on the other hand, when the innovation becomes generally accepted, its originator gets the utmost pleasure as if it were the attainment of his inner desires.'[3] Thus when he made his studies of Dutch and then English language, with its enormous difficulties, when he made the enormous effort to visit and document America and European civilization, he was finding a model for himself, a world where individual freedom was taken for granted as the premise of life, rather than being seen as largely selfish and de-stabilizing. He believed passionately that both for himself and for Japan, this was the only way to go. He himself had discovered this in relation to his clan. At the wider level 'The independence of a nation springs from the independent spirit of its citizens. Our nation cannot hold its own if the old slavish spirit is so manifest among the people.'[4]

Much of the tension and interest in Fukuzawa's work comes out of his rebellious nature. He describes himself as a stubborn and individualistic person by character. 'I was always concerned with the way of society, and it was my inborn nature to act always in my own way.'[5] He speaks of 'my principle of independence and self-help'[6] and of 'My general determination was to be independent, to earn my own way and not to beg, borrow or covet other men's property.'[7]

All this hard work, financial and political independence, planning and ambition makes Fukuzawa sound a dry, two-dimensional person. Indeed he realized himself that his **Autobiography** tended to give this impression. 'It may thus appear that I am a queer bigoted person, but in reality I am quite sociable with all people. Rich or poor, noble or commoner, scholar or illiterate - all are my friends. I have no particular feeling in meeting a **geisha** or any other woman.'[8] Yet even here another vice, philandering lust, is dismissed. Was he perfect, then?

To round out the picture we can note three weaknesses. A small one was a certain absent-mindedness which reminds us of Adam Smith. Fukuzawa related that 'One day when I was suddenly called out on business, I thought of changing

---

[1] Fukuzawa, **Autobiography**, 284
[2] Fukuzawa, **Autobiography**, 286
[3] Fukuzawa, **Autobiography**, 209
[4] Fukuzawa, **Autobiography**, 314
[5] Fukuzawa, **Autobiography**, 11
[6] Fukuzawa, **Autobiography**, 287
[7] Fukuzawa, **Autobiography**, 265
[8] Fukuzawa, **Autobiography**, 292

my dress. My wife being out at the moment, I opened the chest of drawers and took out a garment that happened to be lying on top. When I returned, my wife looked curiously at me and said I was wearing an undergarment. She had one more cause for laughing at me. In this case, of course, my unconcern for dress went a little too near the limit.'[1] The implication is that he was also oblivious to social conventions - a sort of Japanese eccentric.

Nor can we strongly condemn what he himself found an ambivalent attitude to money. While he was full of probity in general, he found that when it came to the assets of his clan, he felt no moral necessity to be strictly honest. 'In the narrative so far I may appear to be a highly upright person in matters of money. But I must admit here that I was not always so. I was quite otherwise when it came to money belonging to my clan.'[2] He proceeded to give a few examples of a different attitude to the joint property of an institution which he already resented strongly.

It was in his leisure activities that we find the one real chink in his puritan character. This was not his fondness for Japanese music, which was not taken to excess. He wrote that 'I have always been fond of music, so much so that I am having all my daughters and granddaughters learn both **koto** and **shamisen** and also, partly for exercise, dancing. To sit and listen to them at their lessons is the chief pleasure of my old age.'[3] His chief weakness, and one which he finally successfully overcame, was drink.

Quite early in his **Autobiography** he wrote as follows. 'To begin with the shortcomings, my greatest weakness lay in drinking, even from my childhood. And by the time I was grown enough to realize its dangers, the habit had become a part of my own self and I could not restrain it. I shall not hold back anything, for however disagreeable it may be to bring out my old faults, I must tell the truth to make a true story. So I shall give, in passing, a history of my drinking from its very beginning.'[4] Towards the end of the same book he returned to the same subject, where he wrote that

> I must admit I have had a very bad and shameful habit of drinking. Moreover, my drinking was something out of the ordinary. There is a kind of drinker who does not really like the wine, and does not think of drinking until he sees the wine brought before him. But I was of the kind who liked it, and wanted much of it, and moreover wanted good, expensive wine. At one time when it cost seven or eight **yen** a barrel, my expert taste could tell the better wine from the less expensive if there was a difference of even fifty **sen**. I used to drink a lot of this good wine, eat plenty of nice food with it and continue devouring bowl after bowl of rice, leaving nothing on the table. Indeed, I was 'drinking like a cow and eating like a horse.'[5]

At about the age of thirty-three he began to realize that this heavy drinking would shorten his life. He remembered an earlier attempt suddenly to give up all drinking and decided to wean himself slowly. 'It was as hard a struggle as a Chinaman giving up his opium. First I gave up my morning wine, then my noon wine. But I always excused myself to take a few cups when there was a guest.

---

[1] Fukuzawa, **Autobiography**, 296
[2] Fukuzawa, **Autobiography**, 271
[3] Fukuzawa, **Autobiography**, 295
[4] Fukuzawa, **Autobiography**, 52
[5] Fukuzawa, **Autobiography**, 326

Gradually I was able to offer the cup to the guest only and keep myself from touching it. So far I managed somehow, but the next step of giving up the evening wine was the hardest of all my efforts.'[1] It took him about three years to give up the habit entirely, but in this, as in other things, we notice the force of his will and reason.

Yet his ability to curb his body and his emotions does not mean that he was a dry or emotionless man. Again and again in his writing his strong feelings flash out, and we see a man driven by anger, shame or admiration. For instance, when describing the sexual behaviour of many of his countrymen he wrote 'For a man, especially one who has been abroad, to fall into such loose behaviour is too much for me to bear.'[2] Or again, the treatment of women, and the way this treatment was viewed by westerners, made him deeply upset. 'I am stunned beyond words at the brazen shamelessness of our people.'[3] It was not that he did not feel, it was more that he channelled this feeling through his writing and practical activities. As he put it, 'the human body and mind are like an iron kettle. If they are not used, they rust.'[4]

---

[1] Fukuzawa, **Autobiography**, 328
[2] Fukuzawa, **Women**, 85
[3] Fukuzawa, **Women**, 200
[4] Fukuzawa, **Women**, 134

4. TRAVELS IN JAPAN, AMERICA AND EUROPE

As he reached the age of fourteen or fifteen Fukuzawa grew increasingly frustrated in the provincial atmosphere of Nakatsu. 'Outwardly I was living peacefully enough, but always in my heart I was praying for an opportunity to get away. And I was willing to go anywhere and to go through any hardship if only I could leave this uncomfortable Nakatsu. Happily, a chance sent me to Nagasaki.'[1] He wrote that a particular event confirmed him in his decision to leave. Fukuzawa's brother had written a letter to the clan's chief minister for which he was reprimanded because it was not properly addressed. 'Seeing this I cried to myself, 'how foolish it is to stay here and submit to this arrogance!' And I was determined then to run away from this narrow cooped-up Nakatsu.'[2]

Fukuzawa's chance to escape was one of the many effects of the first shock of the imminent revolution in Japan. In 1854 Commodore Perry had appeared with the American warships off the coast of Japan and this 'had made its impression on every remote town in Japan.'[3] Thus 'the problem of national defense and the modern gunnery had become the foremost interest of all the samurai.'[4] In order to study western gunnery one had to be able to read Dutch, so Fukuzawa volunteered to do that and, in 1854, at the age of nineteen was taken to Nagasaki to learn Dutch and gunnery. 'The true reason why I went there was nothing more than to get away from Nakatsu....This was a happy day for me. I turned at the end of the town's street, spat on the ground, and walked quickly away.'[5]

He set himself hard to work. 'My chief concern was, after all, the Dutch language. I often went to the interpreter's house, and sometimes to the house of the special physicians who practiced 'Dutch medicine'. And little by little, after fifty or a hundred days, I came to understand something of the Dutch language.'[6] Because of jealousies within the clan,[7] it became difficult to stay in Nagasaki and the following February (1855) he left and ended up a month later as a student at the school of Koan Ogata in Osaka. Ogata was one of the foremost experts on the Dutch learning in Japan.

Fukuzawa gives a delightful and lengthy account of his life as a student with Ogata. Like many of his young contemporaries he became fascinated with western science and technology. For instance he describes how

> Of course at that time there were no examples of industrial machinery. A steam engine could not be seen anywhere in the whole of Japan. Nor was there any kind of apparatus for chemical experiments. However, learning something of the theories of chemistry and machinery in our books, we of the Ogata household [school] spent much effort in trying out what we had learned, or trying to make a thing that was illustrated in the books.[8]

---

[1] Fukuzawa, **Autobiography**, 20
[2] Fukuzawa, **Autobiography**, 19
[3] Fukuzawa, **Autobiography**, 21
[4] Fukuzawa, **Autobiography**, 21
[5] Fukuzawa, **Autobiography**, 22
[6] Fukuzawa, **Autobiography**, 25
[7] Fukuzawa, **Autobiography**, 25-6
[8] Fukuzawa, **Autobiography**, 84

Learning about the new science was not easy. For instance, there was no good work on electricity. 'All that we knew about electricity then had been gleaned from fragmentary mention of it in the Dutch readers.'[1] One day Ogata returned with a Dutch volume borrowed from his clan lord. 'I took in the book with devouring eyes...here in this new book from Europe was a full explanation based on the recent discoveries of the great English physicist, Faraday, even with the diagram of an electric cell. My heart was carried away with it at first sight.'[2] He and his fellow students proceeded to work day and night to copy out the whole long chapter on electricity before returning it. 'This event quite changed the whole approach to the subject of electricity in the Ogata household. I do not hesitate to say that my fellow students became the best informed men on the new science in the entire country.'[3]

Fukuzawa learnt the basics of western chemistry and physics during the years 1856-1860. This partly explains his increasing dislike of Chinese Knowledge. 'The only subject that bore our constant attack was Chinese medicine. And by hating Chinese medicine so thoroughly, we came to dislike everything that had any connection with Chinese culture. Our general opinion was that we should rid our country of the influences of the Chinese altogether.'[4] He came, as he explained later, to see Chinese mis-information as a block to knowledge and advance. 'The true reason of my opposing the Chinese teaching with such vigour is my belief that in this age of transition, if this retrogressive doctrine remains at all in our young men's minds, the new civilization cannot give its full benefit to this country.'[5] In his old age he wrote in his **Old Man Fukuzawa's Tales** that 'I am not one who studies western learning and tries to combine it with Chinese learning. I wish to tear up traditional teaching by the roots and open the way to the new culture. In other words I wish to use one learning to destroy the other and these two things have been my lifelong concerns.'[6]

He worked with huge concentration but great uncertainty. There was no obvious job ahead and much anti-foreign feeling in the country. Like others at Ogata's school, 'most of us were then actually putting all our energy into our studies without any definite assurance of the future. Yet this lack of future hope was indeed fortunate for us, for it made us better students than those in Yedo.'[7]

Then in October 1858 the clan needed a Dutch scholar to open a school in Yedo (Tokyo). He moved there and continued his studies. Yet he was in for a sudden shock. He visited Yokohama in 1859 and noted that 'I had been striving with all my powers for many years to learn the Dutch language. And now when I had reason to believe myself one of the best in the country, I found that I could not even read the signs of merchants who had come to trade with us from foreign lands. It was a bitter disappointment, but I knew it was no time to be downhearted.'[8] The language of the world was English, not Dutch. So 'On the

---

[1] Fukuzawa, **Autobiography**, 88
[2] Fukuzawa, **Autobiography**, 88
[3] Fukuzawa, **Autobiography**, 89
[4] Fukuzawa, **Autobiography**, 91
[5] Fukuzawa, **Autobiography**, 216
[6] Quoted in Kato, **Japanese Literature**, III, 81
[7] Fukuzawa, **Autobiography**, 92
[8] Fukuzawa, **Autobiography**, 98

very next day after returning from Yokohama, I took up a new aim in life and determined to begin the study of English.'[1] He managed to find a two volume Dutch-English dictionary, and 'Once with these at my command, I felt there was hope for my endeavour. I made firm my determination to learn the new language by my own efforts. So day and night I plodded along with the new books for sole companions. Sometimes I tried to make out the English sentences by translating each word into Dutch; sometimes I tried forming an English sentence from the Dutch vocabulary. My sole interest then was to accustom myself to the English language.'[2] He progressed well and the following year published his first book **Kaei Tsugo** (English Vocabulary and Idioms). 'This was not exactly a translation; my work was limited to adding **kana** (Japanese syllabary) to indicate the pronunciation of the English words, a very simple task.'[3]

Cometh the man, cometh the moment. 'The year after I was settled in Yedo - the sixth year of Ansei (1859) - the government of the Shogun made a great decision to send a ship-of-war to the United States, an enterprise never before attempted since the foundation of the empire. On this ship I was to have the good fortune of visiting America.'[4] In January 1860 Fukuzawa and others started from Uraga on the ship Kanrin-maru, reaching San Francisco on February 26 (March 27 by the western calendar). He stayed in America itself for about three weeks and returned by way of Hawaii, to arrive back to the publication of his English dictionary in August.

American was quite literally a new and strange world for him. In his **Autobiography** he gives a few examples of the things that shocked and surprised him. Coming from a neat bamboo and paper culture where nothing was wasted, he was amazed by the wealth and profligacy: 'there seemed to be an enormous waste of iron everywhere. In garbage piles, on the sea-shores - everywhere - I found lying old oil tins, empty cans, and broken tools. This was remarkable for us, for in Yedo, after a fire, there would appear a swarm of people looking for nails in the ashes.'[5] Likewise the furnishings and concepts of cleanliness were entirely different. 'Here the carpet was laid over an entire room - something quite astounding - and upon this costly fabric walked our hosts wearing the shoes with which they had come in from the streets! We followed them in our hemp sandals.'[6] The relative expense of this affluent culture was a shock. 'Then too, I was surprised at the high cost of daily commodities in California. We had to pay a half-dollar for a bottle of oysters, and there were only twenty or thirty in the bottle at that. In Japan the price of so many would be only a cent or two.'[7]

Due to his earlier efforts to understand western science and technology, steam, electricity, physics and chemistry, he was not particularly surprised or impressed by American technology. 'As for scientific inventions and industrial

---

[1] Fukuzawa, **Autobiography**, 98
[2] Fukuzawa, **Autobiography**, 101
[3] Fukuzawa, **Collected Works**, 34
[4] Fukuzawa, **Autobiography**, 104
[5] Fukuzawa, **Autobiography**, 115-6
[6] Fukuzawa, **Autobiography**, 113
[7] Fukuzawa, **Autobiography**, 116

machinery, there was no great novelty in them for me. It was rather in matters of life and social custom and ways of thinking that I found myself at a loss in America.'[1] He was puzzled by the relations between the sexes. A small example was western dancing. Going to a ball he found that the 'ladies and gentlemen seemed to be hopping about the room together. As funny as it was, we knew it would be rude to laugh, and we controlled our expressions with difficulty as the dancing went on.'[2]

Also surprising was the absence of interest in kinship and descendants.

> One day, on a sudden thought, I asked a gentleman where the descendants of George Washington might be. He replied, 'I think there is a woman who is directly descended from Washington. I don't know where she is now, but I think I have heard she is married.' His answer was so very casual that it shocked me. Of course, I knew that America was a republic with a new president every four years, but I could not help feeling that the family of Washington would be revered above all other families. My reasoning was based on the reverence in Japan for the founders of the great lines of rulers - like that for Ieyasu of the Tokugawa family of Shoguns, really deified in the popular mind. So I remember the astonishment I felt at receiving this indifferent answer about the Washington family.[3]

Fukuzawa left America puzzled and intrigued. He had clearly had a good time and made the most of his opportunities. For instance, to the great envy of his companions, he managed not only to have his photograph taken but persuade the fifteen-year old daughter of the photographer to pose with him. 'As I was going to sit, I saw the girl in the studio. I said suddenly, 'Let us have our picture taken together.' She immediately said, 'All right', being an American girl and thinking nothing of it. So she came and stood by me.'[4] He had learnt a little of the customs of the natives, but after only three weeks 'Things social, political, and economic proved most inexplicable.'[5] Other than the photograph of himself, his most significant acquisition was copy of Webster's dictionary, which 'is deemed to have been Fukuzawa's intellectual weapon in understanding modern civilization'.[6]

In 1861, the year after he returned, Fukuzawa was married in traditional Japanese manner, with a go-between, to Toki Kin. She bore him nine children, four sons and five daughters, all of whom grew to adulthood, though twin babies had been born dead. He described how, 'For the next two or three years, I was more occupied with my struggles in studying English than in teaching. Then, in the second year of Bunkyu (1862), a happy opportunity came my way, and I was able to make a visit to Europe with the envoys sent by our government.'[7]

*

---

[1] Fukuzawa, **Autobiography**, 116
[2] Fukuzawa, **Autobiography**, 114
[3] Fukuzawa, **Autobiography**, 116
[4] Fukuzawa, **Autobiography**, 120
[5] Fukuzawa, **Autobiography**, 116
[6] Nishikawa, 'Fukuzawa', 5
[7] Fukuzawa, **Autobiography**, 124

This second voyage took him away from Japan for almost a year, and involved months spent in several European countries. His own summary of the trip is as follows.

> We sailed in December, still the first year of Bunkyu (1861) on an English war vessel, the Odin, sent over for the purpose of conveying our envoy. We called at Hongkong, Singapore and other ports in the Indian Ocean. Then through the Red Sea to Suez where we landed for the railway journey to Cairo in Egypt. After about two days there, we went by boat again across the Mediterranean to Marseilles. From there we continued by the French railways to Paris, stopping a day at Lyons on our way. We were in Paris for about twenty days while our envoys completed negotiations between France and Japan. Next we crossed to England; then to Holland; from Holland to Berlin, the Prussian capital, and then to St. Petersburg in Russia. The return journey was made through France and Portugal, then retracing our course through the Mediterranean and the Indian Ocean, at length we reached Japan after nearly a year of travelling. It was almost the end of the second year of Bunkyu (1862) when we returned.[1]

In fact, according to western chronology, the journey started in January 1862 and Fukuzawa returned in the December of the same year.

The Japanese authorities who sent out this large fact-finding expedition were caught in a dilemma. They wanted the delegation to gather as much information as possible on all aspects of western 'civilization' so that Japan could prepare itself for development. On the other hand, several hundred years of isolation made these same authorities nervous about the possible effects of this new knowledge on members of the expedition. Thus Fukuzawa noted that 'One ridiculous idea held by our embassy was that its members should not meet the foreigners or see the country any more than they had to. We were under the seclusion theory even when we were travelling in a foreign country.' A member of the expedition was to keep a watchful eye and 'This particularly applied to us three translators.'[2] Thus they were accompanied whenever they went out. 'In spite of all these restrictions, however, we were able to see or hear pretty much everything that we wished.'[3]

An amazing new world revealed itself to Fukuzawa's intensely curious eyes. 'Throughout this tour, new and surprising to us were all the things and institutions of civilization. Everywhere we stayed, we had the opportunity of meeting many people and learning much from them.'[4] Again he was neither particularly impressed with, puzzled by nor interested in pursuing matters scientific and technological, about which he could and had read books.

> All the information dealing with the sciences, engineering, electricity, steam, printing, or the processes of industry and manufacture, contained in my book, I did not really have to acquire in Europe. I was not a specialist in any of those technical fields, and even if I had inquired particularly into them, I could have got only a general idea which could more readily be obtained in text books. So in Europe I gave my chief attention to other more immediately interesting things.[5]

---

[1] Fukuzawa, **Autobiography**, 125
[2] Fukuzawa, **Autobiography**, 131
[3] Fukuzawa, **Autobiography**, 132
[4] Fukuzawa, **Collected Works**, 37
[5] Fukuzawa, **Autobiography**, 154

This proved embarrassing at times, for his hosts were under the impression that the Japanese mission, including Fukuzawa, would be most interested in precisely these technological and scientific advances. This had been a problem in America where his kind hosts directed him to the new marvels.

> But on the contrary, there was really nothing new, at least to me. I knew the principle of the telegraphy even if I had not seen the actual machine before; I knew that sugar was bleached by straining the solution with bone-black, and that in boiling down the solution, the vacuum was used to better effect than heat. I had been studying nothing else but such scientific principles ever since I had entered Ogata's school.[1]

Time was short and Fukuzawa was clear both as to what he did not want to spend his time on, and what was important. 'During this mission in Europe I tried to learn some of the most commonplace details of foreign culture' and the 'common matters of daily life directly from the people, because the Europeans would not describe them in books as being too obvious. Yet to us those common matters were the most difficult to comprehend.'[2] He realized that his interests must have been puzzling to his hosts. 'It was embarrassing on both sides and I regretted it, but somehow I managed to escape to other persons whom I had recognized as likely persons to answer my questions on things I had not found in the dictionaries. All my questions were so commonplace, these gentlemen must have felt the conversation to be wasting of time, but to me, the questions were vital and most puzzling.'[3]

He was particularly interested in the working of institutions and associations and in democratic politics. In terms of institutions, he was fascinated but deeply puzzled by things such as hospitals, the postal services, the police. 'For instance, when I saw a hospital, I wanted to know how it was run - who paid the running expenses; when I visited a bank, I wished to learn how the money was deposited and paid out. By similar first-hand queries, I learned something of the postal system and the military conscription then in force in France but not in England.'[4]

He crammed in an enormous amount, mixing observation with continuous questioning and social contacts.

> Then I was given opportunities to visit the headquarters and buildings of the naval and military posts, factories, both governmental and private, banks, business offices, religious edifices, educational institutions, club houses, hospitals - including even the actual performances of surgical operations. We were often invited to dinners in the homes of important personages, and to dancing parties; we were treated to a continual hospitality until at times we returned exhausted to our lodgings.[5]

Blacker describes how during the six weeks in London, the delegation 'attended the Ball of the Civil Service Volunteers in Willis's Rooms, and the Grand Ball given by the Duchess of Northumberland. They paid frequent visits to the International Exhibition. They inspected Woolwich Arsenal and garrison, the

---

[1] Fukuzawa, **Autobiography**, 115
[2] Fukuzawa, **Autobiography**, 133
[3] Fukuzawa, **Collected Works**, 38
[4] Fukuzawa, **Autobiography**, 134
[5] Fukuzawa, **Autobiography**, 131

Zoo, the Houses of Parliament, Buchanan's Archery Warehouse, the Crystal Palace, King's College Hospital, and the boiler factories of Messrs John Penn and Son at Blackheath.' They were also 'taken to the Derby, down a Newcastle coalmine, and over Portsmouth dockyard.'[1]

Other experiences were equally interesting and Fukuzawa's enthusiasm and curiosity are apparent; 'the hospitals, poor houses, schools for the blind and the deaf, institutions for the insane, museums and the expositions, were all new to look at and as I learned their origins and their contributions, every detail of them filled me with admiration and fascination.'[2]

Just as Tocqueville found the alien political forms in America and England both the most intriguing and difficult to understand, likewise Fukuzawa, coming from an even greater distance, found the political systems in Europe puzzling, yet he sensed their importance. Under a heading 'The people and politics of Europe', he wrote that 'Of political situations of that time, I tried to learn as much as I could from various persons that I met in London and Paris, though it was often difficult to understand things clearly as I was yet so unfamiliar with the history of Europe.'[3]

He noted that 'A perplexing institution was representative government'[4] and gave a vignette of his bewilderment in England when he saw the system in action.

> When I asked a gentleman what the 'election law' was and what kind of bureau the Parliament really was, he simply replied with a smile, meaning I suppose that no intelligent person was expected to ask such a question. But these were the things most difficult of all for me to understand. In this connection, I learned that there were bands of men called political parties - the Liberals and the Conservatives - who were always fighting against each other in the government. For some time it was beyond my comprehension to understand what they were fighting for, and what was meant, anyway, by 'fighting' in peace time. 'This man and that man are enemies in the House,' they would tell me. But these 'enemies' were to be seen at the same table, eating and drinking with each other. I felt as if I could not make much of this. It took me a long time, with some tedious thinking, before I could gather a general notion of these separate mysterious facts. In some of the more complicated matters, I might achieve an understanding five or ten days after they were explained to me. But all in all, I learned much from this initial tour of Europe.'[5]

The vast amount of new information he gathered, and the sight of a new world, would provide the foundation for his life's work.

He put down all his observations and summaries of his conversations in a notebook. 'So, whenever I met a person whom I thought to be of some consequence, I would ask him questions and would put down all he said in a notebook ... After reaching home, I based my ideas on these random notes, doing the necessary research in the books which I had brought back, and thus had the

---

[1] Blacker, **Fukuzawa**, 6-7; for a fuller account see Blacker, 'First Japanese Mission'
[2] Fukuzawa, **Collected Works**, 40
[3] Fukuzawa, **Autobiography**, 129
[4] Fukuzawa, **Autobiography**, 134
[5] Fukuzawa, **Autobiography**, 134-5

material for my book, Seiyo Jijo (Things Western).'[1] We are told that 'One of his notebooks has been preserved. It is crammed with information in Japanese, English and Dutch on such varied subjects as the cost per mile of building a railway, the number of students in King's College, London, and the correct process for hardening wood.'[2]

---

[1] Fukuzawa, **Autobiography**, 133; the work is more normally given the translated title of 'Conditions in the West'.
[2] Blacker, **Fukuzawa**, 7

5. THE COMPARATIVE THINKER

Fukuzawa's three foreign visits and his knowledge of Dutch and English gave him an unique vantage point both in relation to his own civilization and understanding the West. As he realized, he had the basis for a double comparison: the 'ancien regime' past of his clan youth, and the post-revolutionary world that was opening up, and the comparison of Japan and the West. In relation to this he summarized his experiences at the end of his life thus:

> My life begun in the restricted conventions of the small Nakatsu clan was like being packed tightly in a lunch box. When once the toothpick of clan politics was punched into the corner of the box, a boy was caught on its end, and before he himself knew what was happening, he had jumped out of the old home. Not only did he abandon his native province but he even renounced the teaching of the Chinese culture in which he had been educated. Reading strange books, associating with new kinds of people, working with all the freedom never dreamed of before, travelling abroad two or three times, finally he came to find even the empire of Japan too narrow for his domain. What a merry life this has been, and what great changes![1]

The experience of rapidly expanding intellectual horizons, where three hundred years of western thought suddenly became available, is beautifully captured in the following reminiscence.

> When we read history, we realise that Nakatsu was but one of three hundred clans which existed during the Tokugawa period, and that the Tokugawa were merely persons who happened to have seized power in the single island of Japan. We see that beyond Japan lie the almost innumerable countries of Asia and the west, whose histories leave evidence of heroes and great men. When we contemplate the works of Napoleon and Alexander, or imagine the erudition of Newton, Watt or Adam Smith, we realise that there are Hideyoshis beyond the seas and that Butsu Sorai was but a small man of learning from the East. When we read even the bare elements of geography and history, our minds must needs be lifted from their old ways of thought. Into what lofty realms will they rise therefore when we look into the theories of the great thinkers of the west, analysing and comparing inquiring into the cause and effects of all things from the organic laws of the physical world to the formless affairs of men. As we ponder deeply on what we read, we experience a state of rapture as though we were transported into a different world. When, from this position, we look back on the world and its phases, governments seem like small compartments of men's affairs, and wars like the games of children.[2]

The changes within Japan itself were immense. 'The opening of the country and the restoration of Imperial rule caused a great revolution never before experienced in our history. It even affected all our customs, education, and industry, and even such details as clothing, food and housing.'[3] Everything was confusion. 'Japanese met Westerners for the first time since the founding of the Japanese islands. It was a sudden leap from the silent depths of night into broad daylight. Everything they saw stupefied their minds; they had no categories for understanding anything.'[4] Everything was questioned.

---

[1] Fukuzawa, **Autobiography**, 333
[2] Fukuzawa, **Kyuhanjo**, 327
[3] Fukuzawa, **Women**, 80
[4] Fukuzawa, **Civilization**, 67

> The fall of the Tokugawa regime of three hundred years' standing gave me the cue, and for the first time I realized that my lord was as human as I, and that it was shameful to treat him as I had. I was not the least surprised to see myself undergoing the transition, refusing even the stipend that the clan had willingly offered me. I did not stop to reason this out at the time, but I am convinced now that the fall of the feudal government was what saved me from my slavish attitude.[1]

In contrast with the might and sophistication of Europe and America, the first temptation was to lose faith in one's culture, or at least to recognize realistically that it had 'fallen behind'.

> As a result of our recent ties with foreigners we have begun to contrast our civilization with theirs. Our inferiority to them on the external technological level is obvious, but our mentality also differs from theirs. Westerners are intellectually vital, are personally well-disciplined, and have patterned and orderly social relations. In our present state, from the economy of the nation down to the activities of single households or individuals, we are no match for them. On the whole, it has been only recently that we have realized Western countries are civilized while we as yet are not, and there is no one who in his heart does not admit this fact.[2]

Japan had been sheltered from all this by the formidable bulk of China, but now China had been humiliated.

> The only trouble with us is that we have had too long a period of peace with no intercourse with outside. In the meanwhile, other countries, stimulated by occasional wars, have invented many new things such as steam trains, steam ships, big guns and small hand-guns etc. We did not know all that, for we did not see anything beyond our borders, the only studies we have had being Chinese books, and the only military arts fencing with swords and spears. Naturally we are finding ourselves very much behind times and fearful of the foreign countries.[3]

The enormity of the changes required were indeed daunting after the long period of seclusion.

> True, we have often been shaken by the changing fortunes of history in our two and a half millennia. But as a force which has shaken the very depths of men's minds, the recent relations with foreigners have been the most powerful single set of events since Confucianism and Buddhism were introduced from China in the distant past. Furthermore, Buddhist and Confucian teachings transmitted Asian ideas and practices. They were different only in degree from Japanese institutions, so they may have been novel, but they were not so very strange to our ancestors. The same cannot be said of relations with foreigners in recent history. We have suddenly been thrust into close contact with countries whose indigenous civilizations differ in terms of geographical location and cultural elements, in the evolution of those cultural elements, and in the degree of their evolution. They are not only novel and exotic for us Japanese; everything we see and hear about those cultures is strange and mysterious. If I may use a simile, a blazing brand has suddenly been thrust into ice-cold water. Not only are ripples and swells ruffling the surface of men's minds, but a massive upheaval is being stirred up at the very depths of their souls.[4]

The difficulty was increased by the speed at which Japan would have to adapt if it were not to follow the path of India and China and Africa and become European colonies.

---

[1] Fukuzawa, **Autobiography**, 276
[2] Fukuzawa, **Civilization**, 172
[3] Fukuzawa, **Collected Works**, 30
[4] Fukuzawa, **Civilization**, 1-2

What are, then, the alarming factors that confront the Japanese people in the Meiji Era? The foreign relations are what they are. In commerce, the foreigners are rich and clever; the Japanese are poor and unused to the business. In courts of law, it so often happens that the Japanese people are condemned while the foreigners get around the law. In learning, we are obliged to learn from them. In finances, we must borrow capital from them. We would prefer to open our society to foreigners in gradual stages and move toward civilization at our own pace, but they insist on the principle of free trade and urge us to let them come into our island at once. In all things, in all projects, they take the lead and we are on the defensive. There hardly ever is an equal give and take.[1]

The enormous gap in every aspect became more and more apparent and the bitterness at the way in which Chinese knowledge had provided such a feeble bulwark is evident in another passage.

If we compare the levels of intelligence of Japanese and Westerners, in literature, the arts, commerce, or industry, from the biggest things to the least, in a thousand cases or in one, there is not a single area in which the other side is not superior to us. We can compete with the West in nothing, and no one even thinks about competing with the West. Only the most ignorant thinks that Japan's learning, arts, commerce, or industry is on a par with that of the West. Who would compare a man-drawn cart with a steam engine, or a Japanese sword with a rifle? While we are expounding on **yin** and **yang** and the Five Elements, they are discovering the sixty-element atomic chart. While we are divining lucky and unlucky days by astrology, they have charted the courses of comets and are studying the constitution of the sun and the moon. While we think that we live on a flat, immobile earth, they know that it is round and in motion. While we regard Japan as the sacrosanct islands of the gods, they have raced around the world, discovering new lands and founding new nations. Many of their political, commercial, and legal institutions are more admirable than anything we have. In all these things there is nothing about our present situation that we can be proud of before them.[2]

So far Fukuzawa was only reflecting what a number of his friends were saying. What makes him great is that he applied his intelligence effectively to doing something about the situation. One thing he did was to move beyond the first realistic assessment of western superiority to a more sober assessment of the weaknesses of that system. He combined enthusiasm for the new world of liberty and democracy, with a knowledge that it was far from perfect. He appeared at times to be advocating a total abandonment of Japanese traditions, writing 'If we are to open our country to the world, we must open it all the way and bring in everything of the West. This is what I have always advocated.'[3] Yet on the very same page he urged selectivity. 'Not every product of the West will be good or useful. But if there is something clearly inferior or bad on our side, then we must without a moment's delay correct it.'[4]

He found the new civilization, especially in America, over-obsessed with material wealth. Although producing many things,

the results of attaining the benefit of the best and the most beautiful have been disappointing. Their men spend their lives in the feverish pursuit of money. The only function of their women is feverishly to breed male heirs to carry on the economic struggle. Can this be called the ideal society? I hardly think so. This observation of Mill suffices to give us some ideas of at least one undesirable aspect of the American character.[5]

---

[1]Fukuzawa, **Collected Works**, 62
[2]Fukuzawa, **Civilization**, 99
[3]Fukuzawa, **Women**, 148
[4]Fukuzawa, **Women**, 148
[5]Fukuzawa, **Civilization**, 44

He also noted that although proclaiming equality, the **de facto** situation was not, perhaps, as good as it was in Japan. 'The civilization of the West is of course to be admired. It has been only recently since we have begun to do so. But it would be better not to believe at all than to do so superficially. The West's wealth and power must truly be envied, but we must not go so far as to imitate the unequal distribution of wealth among her peoples as well.'[1] Likewise, while western nations proclaimed the sovereignty of nations, the rule of international law etc. they behaved with predatory unscrupulousness in their massive imperial expansion into Asia and elsewhere. Individually, many westerners were loutish, aggressive and unpleasant in their dealings with the Japanese. Or again, he noted that 'The taxes of Japan are not light, but if we consider the suffering of the poor people of England because of oppression by the landlord class, we should rather celebrate the happy condition of Japan's farmers. The custom of honouring women in the West is among the finest in the world. But if a wicked wife dominates and plagues her husband, or a disobedient daughter scorns her parents and gives free reign to disgraceful conduct, let us not be intoxicated over the custom.'[2] In summary, the West was far ahead in its material life, its political and social institutions and scientific knowledge, but its ethical foundations were less laudable. 'When I observe the ethical behaviour of Japanese men and compare it with that of men in other civilized countries, I do not find Japanese men inferior.'[3]

Fukuzawa saw his task as combining Western science, technology, and political institutions and a market economy, with the traditional 'spirit' or ethic of historical Japan. That Japan is today such a curious blend of 'West' and 'East' is in no small part due to his clear vision of the problem, for 'the superiority of Western over Japanese civilization is certainly very great, but Western civilization is hardly perfect.'[4]

Fukuzawa's greatness also arises from the fact that he saw himself as a spectator looking at two worlds, both from the outside. In relation to his own Japanese upbringing and world, he had become a sympathetic outsider, participant and then observer.

> A man goes through life as if sailing on the sea in a boat. The men in the boat naturally move with the boat, but they may well be unaware of how fast and in what direction the boat is moving. Only those who watch from the shore can know these things with any accuracy. The samurai of the old Nakatsu clan moved with the clan, but they may have been unaware of how they were moving, and may not realise just how they came to arrive at their present state. I alone have stood, as it were, on the shore of the clan, and, as a spectator, may have had a more accurate view of the samurai within the clan. Hence I have committed my spectator's view to writing.'[5]

Equally interesting is the fact that he could look at western civilization as it reached its greatest period of expansion and technological superiority, from the outside. While people like Mill and Buckle and others could only conjecture what

---

[1] Fukuzawa, **Learning**, 99
[2] Fukuzawa, **Learning**, 99
[3] Fukuzawa, **Women**, 96
[4] Fukuzawa, **Learning**, 95
[5] Fukuzawa, **Kyuhanjo**, 308

a pre-industrial, **ancien regime** world was like, Fukuzawa could re-live in his own lifetime the experience of one hundred and fifty years of dramatic change. Compressed into his single life was the most massive shift which has occurred in human history in the last ten thousand years.

He saw very clearly that this gave him an advantage, the shock of surprise and amazement which is the basis of deep discovery.

> We also have the advantage of being able directly to contrast our own personal pre-Meiji experience with Western civilization. Here we have an advantage over our Western counterparts, who, locked within an already matured civilization, have to make conjectures about conditions in other countries, while we can attest to the changes of history through the more reliable witness of personal experience. This actual experience of pre-Meiji Japan is the accidental windfall we scholars of the present day enjoy. Since this kind of living memory of our generation will never be repeated again, we have an especially important opportunity to make our mark. Consider how all of today's scholars of Western Learning were, but a few years back, scholars of Chinese Learning, or of Shinto or Buddhism. We were all either from feudal samurai families or were feudal subjects. We have lived two lives, as it were; we unite in ourselves two completely different patterns of experience.[1]

He believed that this would give him a peculiarly valid set of insights.

> What kind of insights shall we not be able to offer when we compare and contrast what we experienced in our earlier days with what we experience of Western civilization? What we have to say is sure to be trustworthy. For this reason, despite my personal inadequacies, I have endeavoured in this humble work to put to use my own limited knowledge of Western Learning...my whole purpose has been to take advantage of the present historically unique opportunity to bequeath my personal impressions to later generations.[2]

---

[1] Fukuzawa, **Civilization**, 3
[2] Fukuzawa, **Civilization**, 3

6. THE MAKING OF A NEW JAPAN

For five years after his return from his travels, Fukuzawa mainly worked as a teacher and translator in Edo. This was a time of growing tension and threat to the old order. For instance on one occasion he moved out of the city fearing a British attack. Because of anti-western sentiments, he avoided certain contacts. But his family grew and he settled into writing. In 1866 he published the first volume of **Seiyo Jijo, Things Western**, which sold, in the end, over a quarter of a million copies. He was made a retainer of the Shogun and continued to work as a teacher. Then in January 1867 he went on his third and last overseas expedition, again to America, and returned six months later. Although he comments less on what he learnt from direct observation, he came back with other treasures.

> On my second journey to America, I had received a much larger allowance than on the previous one. With all my expenses being paid by the government, I was able to purchase a good number of books. I bought many dictionaries of different kinds, texts in geography, history, law, economics, mathematics, and every sort I could secure. They were for the most part the first copies to be brought to Japan, and now with this large library I was able to let each of my students use the originals to study. This was certainly an unheard-of convenience - that all students could have the actual books instead of manuscript copies for their use.[1]

This set the trend, he wrote, for the use of American books in Japan over the next ten years.

His innovation here was supplemented by others. In particular he introduced the concept of tuition fees from students, which he had no doubt seen in the West, and this helped him to set up a school, which, when it moved to a new site in April 1868, was the foundation of the first Japanese university, Keio. He continued his teaching and lecturing as the fate of Japan was decided around him, for in 1868 the Tokugawa Shogunate, which had lasted for two and a half centuries, was overthrown by the revived Imperial power, and the Meiji Restoration was effected through a series of pitched battles.

The Emperor partly won because of superior weaponry, and here again Fukuzawa recognized an opportunity. He obtained a copy of a foreign work on rifles which he hoped to translate, but wondered 'Was I not too brazen to think of translating a book on rifles without knowing anything of it?'[2] So with the aid of the book he dismantled and put together a gun, and 'with this experience, I gained much understanding of the rifle and at once took up the translation of the book and published it.' It came out in 1866 and sold many thousands of copies and he later learnt that his translation had helped one of the greatest of Japanese generals, General Murata, who was later to become a world expert on ordnance.

*

The restoration of the Meiji Emperor in 1868 did not, at first sight, look likely to change Japan or Fukuzawa's life very much. The Emperor's supporters had

---
[1] Fukuzawa, **Autobiography**, 199-200
[2] Fukuzawa, **Collected Works**, 44

been, if anything, more xenophobic and traditionalist than those of the Shogun. As far as Fukuzawa could see at first, the new government looked like 'a collection of fools from the various clans got together to form another archaic anti-foreign government which would probably drive the country to ruin through its blunders.'[1] Yet there was a swift change and he and others discovered that they were in fact 'a collection of energetic, ambitious young men prepared to build up a new Japan on thoroughly western lines...'[2] Fukuzawa and his friends began to feel 'as though they were seeing enacted on the stage a play which they themselves had written.'[3] There was now scope for new work and for the widespread dissemination of the old.

There was also a chance to break finally with his clan. For a while in the 1860's Fukuzawa remained, officially, a member of his clan and drew a stipend and obeyed certain orders. His relations with the clan became more strained over time and he started to question the political views of some of his elders. 'Having taken such an attitude, I could hardly enter the politics of the clan, nor seek a career in it. Consequently I lost all thoughts of depending on the favours of other men. Indeed I attached little value on any man or clan.'[4] After the Meiji Restoration he increasingly followed his own inclinations and finally made a stand. 'If this is disagreeable to them, let them dismiss me. I shall obey the order and get out.'[5]

Looking back on the events, he remembered how difficult it had been at the time. 'This lack of attachment to the clan may seem quite creditable now, but in the eyes of my fellow-clansmen it was taken as a lack of loyalty and human sympathy.'[6] He was adamant, however: 'I did not consider the right or wrong of the conflict; I simply said it was not the kind of activity that students should take part in.'[7] Finally 'This argument seemed to dumbfound the officials. My salary was given up, and all official relations between the clan and myself were broken off as I had proposed.'[8] Thus, Fukuzawa was in the odd situation of having created an independent and individual space within a 'small group' society. He used this space to maximum advantage as he launched more fully on his career of writing and teaching.

It is possible to argue that up to about 1870 Fukuzawa had confined his writing mainly to the explanation of technical matters, non-contentious technological and institutional features of the west. For example, the information he collected on his voyages formed the basis of his three volume work titled **Seiyo Jijo** or **Conditions in the West**, published in 1866, 1868 and 1870. The first volume describes in detail a 'number of Western institutions: schools, newspapers, libraries, government bodies, orphanages, museums, steamships, telegraphs'. It then 'gives capsule sketches of the history, government, military systems, and finances of the United States, the

---

[1] Quoted in Blacker, 27.
[2] Blacker, **Fukuzawa**, 28
[3] Blacker, **Fukuzawa**, 28
[4] Fukuzawa, **Autobiography**, 182
[5] Fukuzawa, **Autobiography**, 183
[6] Fukuzawa, **Autobiography**, 183
[7] Fukuzawa, **Autobiography**, 185
[8] Fukuzawa, **Autobiography**, 273

Netherlands and Britain.' The second volume contains 'translations from a popular British series, **Chambers' Educational Course**'. This had been written by John Hill Burton and published by Robert and William Chambers of Edinburgh. 'In this volume, entitled the **Outside Volume** ... the 'corner-stones and main pillars', the intangible social network constituting civilized society, was discussed.'[1] The third volume 'presents general material by Blackstone on human rights and by Wayland on taxes and then supplies historical and other data on Russia and France.'[2]

This technical work was enormously influential, coming just at the moment when Japan was opening to the West. We are told that 'The work exerted a powerful influence on the Japanese public of the time.' The first volume alone sold 150,000 copies, plus over one hundred thousand pirated copies. One of the drafters of the CHARTER OATH and the new proto-constitution for the Meiji restoration wrote that he and his colleagues relied almost exclusively on this work.[3] Fukuzawa was thus not boasting when he gave an account of its impact on his contemporaries.

> At that moment, they came across a new publication called **Seiyo Jijo**. When one person read it and recognized it as interesting and appropriate guide to the new civilization, then a thousand others followed. Among the officials and among the private citizens, whoever discussed Western civilization, obtained a copy of **Seiyo Jijo** for daily reference. This book became the sole authority in its field exactly as the proverb says even a bat can dominate the air where no birds live. Indeed, my book became a general guide to the contemporary society of ignorant men, and some of the decrees issued by the new government seem to have had their origins in this book.[4]

It was the right book at the right time. 'Then, how did it happen that this book became a great power and dominated the whole society of Japan? I reason that this book came upon the right time after the opening of the country when the people, high and low, were feeling lost in the new world.'[5] He had started the work before the Meiji Restoration and the three volumes were completed before the outcome was clear. 'Even if they were to win some attention, I had no idea that the contents of the books would ever be applied to our own social conditions. In short, I was writing my books simply as stories of the West or as curious tales of a dreamland.'[6] Yet the 'dreamland' became the avid focus of Japanese attention and Fukuzawa's ambition increased.

He continued to supply popular and useful works for a westernizing Japan. For example he decided that a rational accounting system was essential for Japan, but first the principles of economics needed to be explained.

> I sat back and thought over the situation, and came upon the idea that the merchants and the men in industry should have been acquainted with the principles of the Western economics before they took up the Western method of business practices. To jump to the reform of their books without this basic knowledge was against the natural order of things. What one should do now would be to teach a wide circle of young men the general and basic principle of

---

[1] From the preface, quoted in Nishikawa, 'Fukuzawa', 6
[2] **Kodansha Encyclopedia**, s.v. **Seiyo jijo**, 54
[3] **Kodansha Encyclopedia**, s.v. 'Seiyo Jijo' 54
[4] Fukuzawa, **Collected Works**, 41
[5] Fukuzawa, **Collected Works**, 41
[6] Fukuzawa, **Autobiography**, 334

Western economics and wait till they grow up and take over the business. After that, the practical value of the new bookkeeping will be realized. With this idea in my mind what I produced in a textbook style was this **Minkan Keizairoku**.[1]

He then produced the follow-up, the book on accounting, admitting, as he had done with his book on rifles, that it was one thing to explain the principles, another to be able to use them.

> In the early years of the Restoration I translated a book on the methods of bookkeeping, and I know that all the correct texts follow the example of my book. So I should know something of the practice, if not enough to be an expert. But apparently the brains of a writer of books and those of a business man are different; I cannot put my bookkeeping into use. I even have great difficulty in understanding the files which other people make.'[2]

The early 1870s saw a rapid shift in the level of his work as he recognized that his mission was not merely to explain and help introduce science, technology and institutional structures (for instance he helped to lay the foundations of a western-style police force)[3], but, much more difficult, to change culture and ideology. He set about trying to introduce the 'spirit' of the West, that is the concepts of liberty, equality and democracy. Thus the 1870s saw the publication of his major philosophical works heavily influenced by Guizot, Mill and Buckle, and hence stemming from the French and Scottish Enlightenment.

In 1872 he started modestly with **A Junior Book of Morals** and then over the next four years wrote the pieces which would constitute one of his major works, the **Encouragement of Learning**. This constituted seventeen pamphlets which came out over the period 1872 to 1876 which, because of their simplicity of style and stringent criticisms of the Tokugawa world, sold enormously well, reaching over 3,400,000 copies.[4] In 1875 he synthesized much of his speculation into an **Outline of Civilization** and the following year published a book close to one of Tocqueville's main themes, **On Decentralization of Power**. Three years later he wrote a **Popular Discourse on People's Rights** and also **A Popular Discourse on National Rights**. These two last books are at the turning point when, for reasons to be discussed below, Fukuzawa's growing distrust of the imperial ambitions of the West led him into a mood of aggressive nationalism which lasted until the defeat of China in 1895. After 1878, he contributed little more that has been widely influential, apart from his **Autobiography**, written in 1899.

Fukuzawa described his writing (with a brush, Japanese fashion) as only one of his two major weapons. 'Consequently I renewed activities with 'tongue and brush', my two cherished instruments. On one side I was teaching in my school and making occasional public speeches, while on the other I was constantly writing on all subjects. And these comprise my books subsequent to Seiyo Jijo. It was a pretty busy life but no more than doing my bit, or 'doing the ten thousandth part' as we put it.'[5]

---

[1] Fukuzawa, **Collected Works**, 90
[2] Fukuzawa, **Autobiography**, 282-3
[3] Fukuzawa, **Autobiography**, 219
[4] Blacker, **Fukuzawa**, 11.
[5] Fukuzawa, **Autobiography**, 335

He was also involved in publishing. He founded the daily newspaper **Jiji Shimpo** in which many of his writings appeared after 1882, and from time to time published his own writings. So successful were all his writing and publishing efforts that 'at that time all works about the West came to be popularly known as **Fukuzawa-bon**.'[1]

Yet the teaching and speech-making were equally important. Here also he was a pioneer and had to invent traditions which were taken for granted in the West. For example, the art of speech-making was something which he had witnessed in the West, but was totally absent in Japan. He gives a graphic account of the background that led up to the publication of his book **Kaigiben** (How to Hold a Conference) in 1873. His account again illustrates his problems and inventiveness when introducing new concepts.

He noted that

> The actuality today is that people hold no wonder over the practice of a man speaking out his own thoughts and communicating them to a group of listeners. Even the technique of shorthand writing has been developed for everyday use. In such a world, some people are liable to feel that the public speaking is a customary art of many centuries. But the fact is that the public speaking was a new and a strange art only twenty odd years ago, and those who endeavoured at it for the first time experienced some untold trials.[2]

Thus he decided to give the history of its introduction into Japan.

In 1873 a colleague

> came to my residence with a small book in English and said that in all the countries in the West, the 'speech' was considered a necessary art in all departments of human life; there was no reason why it was not needed in the Japanese society; rather, it was urgently needed, and because we didn't have it, we were sorely deficient in communicating our thoughts from man to man in politics, in learning and in commerce and industry; there was no telling what our losses were from the inevitable lack of understanding between parties; this present book was on the art of speech; how would it be to make the content of this book known to all our countrymen?[3]

So Fukuzawa, who had already seen the practice at work in England and puzzled over confrontational politics, looked into the matter.

> I opened the book and I found it was indeed a book introducing an entirely new subject to us. 'Then, without further ado, let us translate its general content', I said. I completed in a few days a summary translation, and it is this **Kaigiben**. In the translation, I was met with the problem of finding a proper Japanese word for 'speech'. Then an old recollection came to me that in my Nakatsu Clan, there was a custom of presenting a formal communication to the Clan government on one's personal matter or on one's work. It was not a report or a petition but an expression of one's thoughts, and this communication was called **enzetsu** letter. I have no knowledge as to the customs in other Clans. But as I remembered this word clearly from my Nakatsu days, I discussed it with my colleagues and decided on it as the translated word for 'speech'.[4]

---

[1] Blacker, **Fukuzawa**, 27
[2] Fukuzawa, **Collected Works**, 80
[3] Fukuzawa, **Collected Works**, 80-1
[4] Fukuzawa, **Collected Works**, 81

The word he invented became incorporated into national life and without word and concept modern democracy could not have developed in Japan. 'At present, the speech has become an important element in the National Diet and in all occasions of our lives even in small villages in the countryside. But this word, **enzetsu**, traces its origin to a custom in Nakatsu Clan of Buzen Province, chosen by the members of Keio Gijuku, and then it spread to the rest of the country. Other words such as 'debate' was translated **toron**, 'approve' **kaketsu** and 'reject' **hiketsu**.'[1] Fukuzawa had once again thought things through, and a combination of his wide experience and independence of mind had led to a new conclusion. Although all his friends and colleagues said speech-making was impossible in the Japanese language, 'But when I stopped and thought about it, I came to think that there is no reason why it is not possible to make a speech in Japanese. The reason for the difficulty must be that we Japanese people have not been used to making speeches since olden times. But if you don't try it because of the difficulty, it will stay difficult forever.'[2] We are told that 'He himself demonstrated beautifully the art of public speaking in the presence of sceptics and built a public speaking hall at Keio where he, his fellows and students, held many gatherings and speaking contests'.[3]

The hall is called the Enzetsukan, and survives in a re-built form.

Yet the change that needed to be effected was much deeper than a question of the art of public speaking. Speech itself was much more embedded and socially controlled in Japan than in the west. This made rational, impersonal, speeches very difficult. Speech, as well as gestures and postures, altered dramatically depending on whom one was speaking to. Fukuzawa carried out various experiments to show how strong was this absence of personal consistency and stability. For instance, 'it showed that they were merely following the lead of the person speaking to them.'[4] Much of his effort to teach the Japanese the art of public debate and public speech-making tried to deal with this problem. The desire for approval, to fit in, made it very difficult for people to state an absolute opinion as their own, to take a stand, to argue forcefully and consistently. Everything tended to slip towards the social context. The individual and his views did not matter: he or she must submit to group harmony, sacrifice all individual will to the group. This was built into the language, the bowing, the political and kinship system.

Another part of the problem was that people found it impossible to separate their words and their feelings. As we saw, during his travels he was amazed at the way in which politicians in England could attack each other in the House for their ideas, without any personal animus. The art of debate seemed to be a kind of elaborate game, like a legal confrontation, but it made it possible to separate ideas from their social context and, in other words, allowed 'reason' to prevail.

---

[1] Fukuzawa, **Collected Works**, 81
[2] Fukuzawa, **Collected Works**, 82
[3] Nishikawa, 'Fukuzawa', 8
[4] Fukuzawa, **Autobiography**, 246

More generally, the very concept of allowing political parties to express their dissent, or even exist, was alien to the Japanese tradition. Thus 'in political practices in Japan, a group of more than three to make agreements among themselves privately was called 'conspiracy', and the **kosatsu** (the official bulletin board on the street for announcing government decrees) pronounced that conspiracy was an offence, and indeed it was one of the gravest of offences.'[1] Yet he saw something very puzzlingly different on his visit to Europe. There 'in England I heard that there were what they called 'political parties' and they openly and legally made games of fighting for the supremacy.' When he first encountered this he wondered 'Did that mean that in England, people were permitted to argue and to make attacks on the government decrees and they were not punished?' How could such a system not lead to anarchy? 'Under such untidy condition, it was a wonder that England preserved her internal peace and order.' But he persisted in his observations and questions until 'I felt I was grasping the basis of the English Parliament, the relation between the Royalty and the Parliament, the power of popular opinion and the customs of Cabinet changes - or, did I really grasp them? All the human affairs were baffling.'[2] In his writings he worked through the system of democracy and explained it to himself and his Japanese audience.

Another part of the problem in Japan was that there were no rules of procedure for meetings. 'From the earliest times in Japan, whenever people have assembled to discuss some problem, nothing could be settled because of the lack of any set rules for discussion. This has always been true of disputes among scholars, of business conferences, and of municipal meetings.'[3] All this has to be learnt from a civilization in western Europe which has developed on the basis of Greek philosophy and Western jurisprudence, a complex set of procedures to make decisions and sift out the best arguments.

Even if all these things could be changed, there were other practical problems. There were not even places in which conferences, speeches, or lectures could take place. So Fukuzawa set about physically building the first lecture hall in Japan. Speaking of what would become Keio University, he wrote 'I returned to my school and at once commenced on the plan for introducing the new art to the whole country. The first necessity, we decided, was an auditorium, and that became our first undertaking.'[4] The experiment was a success. Here again he brought in an institution which had been absent in Japan for at least a thousand years. He recognized that western invention and success did not come out of the blue. Selecting the University of Glasgow in the later eighteenth century as his model, he reminded his audience that 'When Watt invented the steam engine and Adam Smith first formulated the laws of economics, they did not sit alone in the dark and experience an instantaneous enlightenment. It was because of long years of studying physical sciences that they were able to achieve their results.'[5] He himself had escaped from his Nakatsu background through the educational

---

[1] Collected Works, 38
[2] Collected Works, 38
[3] Fukuzawa, **Speeches**, 21
[4] Fukuzawa, **Collected Works**, 87
[5] Fukuzawa, **Civilization**, 91

path and much of his later life was devoted to the Baconian project of the 'Advancement', or as Fukuzawa put it, the 'Encouragement' of Learning.

Indeed, it is clear that a part of Fukuzawa's enthusiasm for western-style education lay in his belief that it was a very powerful force in the fight against inequality. He shows this in particular in his account of the history of his Nakaktsu clan after the Meiji Restoration. He describes the fortuitous coming together of events as follows.

> It was owing to this entirely fortuitous stroke of good luck that the Nakatsu clan was able to escape the disasters which fell upon most of the other clans at the time of the Restoration. Later something happened to consolidate this stroke of fortune: namely the establishment of the Municipal School. About the time of the abolition of the clans in 1871 the men who had held official positions in the old clan conferred with the staff of Keiogijuku in Tokyo and decided to divide up the hereditary stipend of the old clan governor and amalgamate it with the savings of the old clan to form a capital fund for promoting Western studies. They then built a school in the old castle town which they called the Municipal School. The rules of the School stipulated that all pupils were to be treated alike, irrespective of their birth or rank - a policy which was not only proclaimed in theory but also carried out in practice. This principle held good from the very day the School was founded, so that it was just as if a new world of equal rights for all people had appeared in the midst of the fading dream of feudal privilege. Many of the staff of Keiogijuku had been samurai of the old Nakatsu clan but they had never interfered in any way with the clan administration, and through all the various disturbances which the clan had undergone had merely looked on with calm hostility.'[1]

The school exercised a magical effect. 'As soon as they really put their hearts into the School they lost all their old notions of birth and rank.'[2] Thus future generations would avoid the bitter memories of his own childhood. 'Whether it be due to mere luck or to a recognizable cause, it is certainly clear that today one sees no trace of resentment or ill-feeling between the clan samurai.'[3] Independence of mind, curiosity, and the treating of all mankind (including women) as born equal, these were the values which Fukuzawa saw as the foundations of his educational work.

---

[1] Fukuzawa, 'Kyuhanjo', 323-4
[2] Fukuzawa, 'Kyuhanjo', 324
[3] Fukuzawa, 'Kyuhanjo', 325

7. COMBINING WESTERN SCIENCE & EASTERN SPIRIT

Fukuzawa's work was centrally concerned with the question of how it would be possible to make Japan rapidly as wealthy and militarily strong as possible. His concern with wealth lay in the growing confrontation between Europe and America on the one hand and Asia on the other. The tiny island of England had humiliated the mighty Chinese Empire in the Opium Wars in 1839-42. Then in 1853 and 1854 the 'black ships' of America had sailed into a Japanese harbour and shown up the hollow weakness of the Japanese Empire. He lamented the fact that 'In general, we Japanese seem to lack the kind of motivation that ought to be standard equipment in human nature. We have sunk to the depths of stagnation.'[1]

Fukuzawa became increasingly aware of the menace of European expansion. He noted that 'In China, for instance, the land is so vast that the interior has as yet to be penetrated by the white man, and he has left his traces only along the coast. However, if future developments can be conjectured, China too will certainly become nothing but a garden for Europeans.'[2] This had already happened in the once mighty civilization of India, and Fukuzawa feared that if India and soon China became provinces of Europe, then Japan would go the same way. The effects would be disastrous. 'Wherever the Europeans touch, the land withers up, as it were; the plants and the trees stop growing. Sometimes even whole populations have been wiped out. As soon as one learns such things and realizes that Japan is also a country in the East, then though we have as yet not been seriously harmed by foreign relations we might well fear the worst is to come.'[3] As the century progressed he felt the increasing menace; if one succumbed, one became a slave; if one competed, one was an outcaste. He noted that 'the whole world is dominated by Western civilization today, and anyone who opposes it will be ostracized from the human society; a nation, too, will find itself outside the world circle of nations.'[4]

His aim was to help turn Japan into a country that was as wealthy as the new industrial nations of the West - and out of this wealth as militarily powerful. He wrote that 'The final purpose of all my work was to create in Japan a civilized nation as well equipped in the arts of war and peace as those of the Western world. I acted as if I had become the sole functioning agent for the introduction of Western learning.'[5] Elsewhere Fukuzawa defined the purpose of his work as follows. 'After all, the purpose of my entire work has not only been to gather young men together and give them the benefit of foreign books but to open this 'closed' country of ours and bring it wholly into the light of Western civilization. For only thus may Japan become strong in the arts of both war and peace and take a place in the forefront of the progress of the world.'[6]

---

[1] Fukuzawa, **Civilization**, 160
[2] Fukuzawa, **Civilization**, 189
[3] Fukuzawa, **Civilization**, 189
[4] Fukuzawa, **Women**, 79
[5] Fukuzawa, **Autobiography**, 214
[6] Fukuzawa, **Autobiography**, 246-7

The essential point was to preserve political independence through economic wealth and military power. He believed that 'foreign relations in our country are a critical problem, from the standpoint both of economics and of power and rights', subservience to foreign powers 'is a deep-seated disease afflicting vital areas of the nation's life.'[1] At times he states that independence is the end, and 'civilization' the means. 'The only reason for making the people in our country today advance toward civilization is to preserve our country's independence. Therefore, our country's independence is the goal, and our people's civilization is the way to that goal.'[2] At other times he saw independence and civilization as synonymous; 'a country's independence equals civilization. Without civilization independence cannot be maintained.'[3]

He realized that Japan and Asia had a long way to go in order to 'catch up'. He found that when he compared 'Occidental and Oriental civilizations' in a 'general way as to wealth, armament, and the greatest happiness for the greatest number, I have to put the Orient below the Occident'.[4] Yet he believed that 'it would not be impossible to form a great nation in this far Orient, which would stand counter to Great Britain of the West, and take an active part in the progress of the whole world.' This was 'my second and greater ambition.'[5]

In these ambitions Fukuzawa was a central figure in the wider Japanese 'Enlightenment', which sought to make Japan both more powerful and more content. Thus he was a founder member of the school of historiography which was 'known as **bummeishiron** (history of civilization) - so called because its chief purpose was to discover from the past the answers pertaining to the nature of civilization: what exactly was civilization and how did it come to be what it is?'[6] Part of his immense popularity and influence arose out of his realization that he was reflecting a national mood. The 'arrival of the Americans in the 1850s has, as it were, kindled a fire in our people's hearts. Now that it is ablaze, it can never be extinguished.' Combined with the later overthrow of the Shogunate and Meiji Restoration of 1868, events 'have become spurs prodding the people of the nation forward. They have caused dissatisfaction with our civilization and aroused enthusiasm for Western civilization. As a result, men's sights are now being reset on the goal of elevating Japanese civilization to parity with the West, or even of surpassing it.'[7]

In order to do this, it was not enough to introduce isolated bits of western technology, to follow China in buying weapons from the West, for instance. It was essential that Japan learnt the principles or spirit behind the technology and created the appropriate institutional structures. 'The idea seems to be that, if England has one thousand warships, and we too have one thousand warships, then we can stand against them.' This was not enough. It was 'the thinking of men who are ignorant of the proportions of things.' Much more was needed. 'If there are one thousand warships, there have to be at least ten thousand

---

[1] Fukuzawa, **Civilization**, 189
[2] Fukuzawa, **Civilization**, 193
[3] Fukuzawa, **Civilization**, 195
[4] Fukuzawa, **Autobiography**, 214-5
[5] Fukuzawa, **Autobiography**, 334
[6] Blacker, **Fukuzawa**, 93
[7] Fukuzawa, **Civilization**, 2

merchant ships, which in turn require at least one hundred thousand navigators; and to create navigators there must be naval science.' Even more than this was required. 'Only when there are many professors and many merchants, when laws are in order and trade prospers, when social conditions are ripe - when, that is, you have all the prerequisites for a thousand warships - only then can there be a thousand warships.'[1]

Fukuzawa was particularly proud that the Japanese seemed to have the ability to assimilate amazingly quickly the art of making and using things, not just buying them:

> it was only in the second year of Ansei (1855) that we began to study navigation from the Dutch in Nagasaki; by 1860, the science was sufficiently understood to enable us to sail a ship across the Pacific. This means that about seven years after the first sight of a steamship, after only about five years of practice, the Japanese people made a trans-Pacific crossing without help from foreign experts.[2]

Yet even this was not enough. He wrote that the '

> civilization of a country should not be evaluated in terms of its external forms. Schools, industry, army and navy, are merely external forms of civilization. It is not difficult to create these forms, which can all be purchased with money. But there is additionally a spiritual component, which cannot be seen or heard, bought or sold, lent or borrowed. Yet its influence on the nation is very great. Without it, the schools, industries, and military capabilities lose their meaning. It is indeed the all-important value, i.e. the spirit of civilization, which in turn is the spirit of independence of a people.[3]

It was essential to change institutions and ideology first, and then the material forms would follow. 'The cornerstone of modern civilization will be laid only when national sentiment has thus been revolutionized, and government institutions with it. When that is done, the foundations of civilization will be laid, and the outward forms of material civilization will follow in accord with a natural process without special effort on our part, will come without our asking, will be acquired without our seeking.' [4] This 'spirit' of civilization had to be understood and then transferred to Japan. This was an immensely difficult task, but one to which he devoted his life.

What he wanted to bring in were not just the **techniques** of the West, but the 'civilization' of the West. He defined this central concept as follows. 'What, then, does civilization mean? I say that it refers to the attainment of **both** material well-being **and** the elevation of the human spirit.'[5] As he began to learn more about the West, first through his book learning, then from his visits to America and Europe, he realized how very different the 'civilization' of Asia and the West were and it was this that puzzled and intrigued him. 'With regard to a nation as a whole, it may be called 'a nation's ways' or 'national opinion'. These things are what is meant by the spirit of civilization. And it is this spirit of civilization that differentiates the manners and customs of Asia and Europe.'[6]

---

[1] Fukuzawa, **Civilization**, 192
[2] Fukuzawa, **Autobiography**, 110
[3] Fukuzawa, **Learning**, 30
[4] Fukuzawa, **Civilization**, 18
[5] Fukuzawa, **Civilization**, 37
[6] Fukuzawa, **Civilization**, 17

Fukuzawa's writings were part of a general 'Enlightenment' movement known as **Keimo**, meaning literally 'enlightening the darkness of the masses'. It was based on a proposition which linked it directly to the European Enlightenment. This was that there was a strong and necessary association between three things, wealth, liberty and equality. We are told that there was agreement among Japanese scholars of the West in the nineteenth century that 'the spiritual secret of the strength and wealth of the western nations lay in the fact that their people were equal and therefore free. It was because the western peoples enjoyed freedom and equal rights and were hence imbued with the spirit of enterprise, initiative and responsibility that the western nations had succeeded in becoming strong, rich and united."[1] For example, 'In the preface to his translation of Smiles' **Self-Help**, published in 1871, Nakamura Keiu stated boldly that the reason why the western nations were strong was not that they possessed armies, but that they possessed the spirit of liberty.'[2] What the Japanese nation needed to learn was the 'spirit of independence, initiative and responsibility such as characterised a people enjoying freedom and equal rights…'[3]

Thus the key questions for Fukuzawa became those of liberty and equality and how they were to be encouraged. His own personal experience in pre-Meiji Japan gave him especial insights into the vast change required, and it is fascinating to see the way in which all of his work is in a sense an autobiography, an externalization of his own struggle to move from lack of freedom to liberty, and from hierarchy to equality.

*

The shift towards a more nationalistic and chauvinistic attitude between about 1875 and 1895 is obvious. Carmen Blacker describes his shifting views in some detail. She quotes him as writing in 1878 that "International law and treaties of friendship have high-sounding names, it is true, but they are nothing more than external, nominal forms. In fact international relations are based on nothing more than quarrels over power and profit…A few cannons are worth more than a hundred volumes of international law. A case of ammunition is of more use than innumerable treaties of friendship."[4] There is much more to this effect and in the following year he wrote "A nation does not come out on top because it is in the right. It is right because it has come out on top."[5] He saw the senselessness of it all, but what was one to do? "All this may be useless and stupid, but when others treat one stupidly one can only do the same back to them. When others use violence, we must be violent too. When others use deceitful trickery we must do likewise."[6] He asked "Have the European countries really respected the rights and interests and integrity of the countries with which they have come into contact? What about Persia? And India? And Siam? And Luzon and Hawaii?…Wherever the Europeans come, the land ceases to be productive, and trees and plants cease to grow. Worse still, the human race

---

[1] Blacker, **Fukuzawa**, 30
[2] Blacker, **Fukuzawa**, 30
[3] Blacker, **Fukuzawa**, 32
[4] Blacker, **Fukuzawa**, 129
[5] Blacker, **Fukuzawa**, 130
[6] Blacker, **Fukuzawa**, 130

sometimes dies out."¹ Japan should 'join' the West and behave as western countries did. In an article in 1885 he wrote that 'Our immediate policy, therefore, should be to lose no time in waiting for the enlightenment of our neighbouring countries (Korea and China) in order to join them in developing Asia, but rather to depart from their rank and cast our lot with the civilized countries of the West... We should deal with them exactly as the Westerners do.'²

Fukuzawa also noted the arrogance of foreigners in Japan. "They eat and drink, and then leave without paying. They ride in **rikishas** without paying. They accept payment in advance for a contract, and then fail to deliver the goods...Not only are they grasping about money; they often break laws and offend against propriety."³ Blacker notes that his earlier praise of democratic and balanced polities, and of individual rights, was almost abandoned for a few years as he became an autocratic nationalist and quasi-imperialist. She quotes him as writing in 1882 that the 'one object of my life is to extend Japan's national power... Even if the government be autocratic in name and form, I shall be satisfied with it if it is strong enough to strengthen the country."⁴ This, of course, ran right against many of his liberal statements, for instance that 'For true human beings to be treated like instruments is an insult, for the honour and dignity of human beings is disregarded and makes death preferable to life.'⁵ Yet it is clear that he had indeed switched. 'If Fukuzawa's sudden neglect of people's rights in favour of national strength at this period might appear illiberal, the policy he recommended Japan to adopt towards the other Asiatic countries was frankly imperialistic.'⁶ It was Japan's duty to become the leader of Eastern Asia and, if necessary, invasion of neighbouring states was justified. His 'nationalistic sentiments reached their climax during the Sino-Japanese War', which he vigorously supported.⁷

Albert Craig argues even more strongly that Fukuzawa lost his faith in the law of nations and natural rights for a considerable period. Thus 'By 1881 Fukuzawa's disillusionment with the morality of natural law had become even more profound. He retained the ideal of civilization as a noble concept, but he denied it any real grounding in nature.'⁸ Craig quotes extensively from some of his writings. "Laws are made for evil men, as medicine is for the diseased. **Millions** of years hereafter, when disease has vanished and all men are good, laws and medicine may be abandoned. In the meantime it is useless to speak of popular rights based on nature (**tennen no minkenron**); they are not worth discussing."⁹ He became increasingly cynical. In 1881 he asked '

> Do nations... honour treaties? We can find not the slightest evidence that they do... When countries break treaties ... there are no courts to judge them. Therefore, whether a treaty is honoured or not... depends solely on the financial and military powers of the countries involved... **Money and soldiers are not for the protection of existing principles**

---

¹ Blacker, **Fukuzawa**, 131
² Nishikawa, 'Fukuzawa', 13
³ Blacker, **Fukuzawa**, 132
⁴ Blacker, Fukuzawa, 134
⁵ Fukuzawa, Women, 50
⁶ Blacker, **Fukuzawa**, 135
⁷ Blacker, **Fukuzawa**, 137
⁸ Craig, 126
⁹ Quoted in Craig, 126

they are the instruments for the creation of principles where none exist. ...in my opinion the Western nations ... are growing ever stronger in the skills of war. In recent years every country devises strange new weapons. Day by day they increase their standing armies. This is truly useless, truly stupid. Yet if others work at being stupid, then I must respond in kind. If others are violent, then I must become violent...Those of my persuasion follow the way of force.[1]

Like Blacker, Craig believes that in this period, 'much of the liberal content of his earlier thought slowly seeped away.'[2] He argues that in this period 'there was nothing other to turn to than the spiritual power of the emperor or the residues of irrational samurai morality.'[3] Although Fukuzawa still 'favoured cultural diversity and political pluralism', for a time he felt that 'Japan, at its stage of civilization, could not handle these things without grave internal disturbances. Fukuzawa foresaw that instant constitutional government in a developing nation could lead to violent rifts in the national consensus, which in turn might destroy constitutional government and bring dictatorship.' Thus for a time 'he stressed the emperor, who alone could make Japan strong and united while advancing toward full constitutional government.' At this period 'Fukuzawa spoke more of duties and less of rights, more of science and less of freedom.'[4]

It is not difficult to see how the world must have looked to someone on the edge of the rapid advance of western imperialism and capitalism as it swept across Asia. On his visit to Europe he had seen 'the miserable conditions of the native people living under western colonialism during stopovers in British Ceylon and Hong Kong. He realized that advanced western countries ruled the poor nations of Asia under the principal of 'might is right'.'[5] For a while the ability of Japan to withstand colonialization hung in the balance. Proof that it could do so was afforded by the victory of the Japanese over the Chinese in 1895. As Fukuzawa wrote,

> The Sino-Japanese War is the victory of a united government and people. There are no words that can express my pleasure and thankfulness: to experience such an event is what life is for... In truth the Sino-Japanese War does not amount to much; it is but a prelude to Japan's future diplomacy, and is no occasion for such rejoicing. Yet I am so overcome by emotions that I enter a dreamlike state... The strength, wealth, and civilization of the new Japan are all due to the virtues of those who went before.[6]

Craig comments that 'Victory in war removed the load of Japan from Fukuzawa's shoulders. No longer was it necessary for him to talk up the national spirit or warn the people of present perils... he began again to talk of the larger philosophical issues of ethics and cosmology that had occupied his attentions during the early 1870's.'[7]

It is clear that 'civilization' and political independence were always inextricably linked in Fukuzawa's thought. If he became cynical about the motivations of the western powers and came to believe that all their preaching of

---

[1] Quoted in Craig, 128-9, emphasis added by Craig
[2] Craig, 129
[3] Craig, 147
[4] Craig, 135
[5] Yaskukawa, 'Fukuzawa Yukichi', 21-2. See also pp.29-36 for further evidence of his nationalist ideas.
[6] Quoted in Craig, 136; cf. the same passage in Autobiography, 335
[7] Craig, 136

natural rights and the dignity of man conflicted with their predatory behaviour, he had good cause to be alarmed. It is indeed part of his interest that he reflected on those very issues of trying to combine democratic and liberal ideals with **realpolitik** which face many developing nations today.

*

Fukuzawa's life spanned the period from the first great work of Tocqueville in 1835, to the middle of the career of Max Weber in 1901. He had witnessed two great discontinuities. Through his travels he had seen the huge gap that had developed between East and West by the 1850s. In the 1860s and 1870s he had seen a revolution from the **ancien regime** of the Tokugawa to the new Meiji world, a change greater even than that witnessed by Tocqueville. Developments which had taken over two hundred years in the West occurred in a decade in Japan. He recognized the central revolution which had taken place, and he realized that in many ways his task was to understand the implications of that change for Japan - namely the scientific, industrial, economic and political revolutions of early modern Europe. Thus he wrote, 'Take the history of any Western country and read about it from its beginning up to the 1600s. Then skip the next two hundred years, and pick up the story again from around 1800. So astonishing will have been the leap forward in that country's progress that we can hardly believe it is the official history of the same country.'[1] Yet he also stressed continuity. 'Inquiring further into the cause of its progress, we will find that it has been due to the legacy and gifts of those who went before them.'[2] This was vitally important for Japan. Not all that had existed in its great civilization of a thousand years or more was useless. The new world should also build on the legacy of the past, including the Imperial tradition and the ethic of his samurai antecedents.

So, at the end of his life, when Fukuzawa looked back, his far-off youth, and his travels to America and Europe, felt very distant. The changes had been immense. 'Sixty-odd years is the length of life I have now come through. It is often the part of an old man to say that life on looking back seems like a dream. But for me it has been a very merry dream, full of changes and surprises.'[3] He felt he had 'nothing to complain of on looking backward, nothing but full satisfaction and delight.'[4]

---

[1] Fukuzawa, **Learning**, 60
[2] Fukuzawa, **Learning**, 60
[3] Fukuzawa, **Autobiography**, 333
[4] Fukuzawa, **Autobiography**, 335

8. METHODS IN THE STUDY OF CIVILIZATION

It is one thing to have seen a new world and to wish to bring its best features to an old one. It is quite another to explain what one has seen in terms that make it comprehensible and attractive. Here we find another part of Fukuzawa's genius. Like all the great thinkers I have considered, he devoted special attention to style and rhetoric. Montesquieu wrote and re-wrote everything with great care, Adam Smith attempted a very clear and simple style, as did Tocqueville, trying out all his writing on close friends. It was important for them to be widely understood. It is thus interesting to find the same pre-occupation with style and writing in Fukuzawa. Again in his case there is perhaps even more attention to the matter for he faced problems which were much greater than his European mentors, as we shall see.

In his early days Fukuzawa was given very good advice by his teacher Ogata.

At that time, I was engaged in translation of a book on fortification by a Dutch man named C.M.H. Pel. One day, Ogata Sensei gave me a kind advice, saying: 'The book you are translating is for the use of the **samurai**. If **samurais** are to be your target, be careful in the use of the Chinese characters. Never use any difficult character or words, because most of them are poor in scholarship and for them high-flown words are tabu. Take the average of the **samurais** you know, you would find yourself high above the average though you are still young and not a scholar of Chinese classics. And so, your effort in decorating your translation with high-sounding words will simply add to the difficulties for the reader. Use only those words and characters you know. Never look in a dictionary for grander words. Such dictionaries as '**Gyokuhen**' and '**Zatsuki Ruihen**' you should never keep near your desk.'[1]

Fukuzawa took this to heart. 'While writing, whenever a rare word began to appear at my pen point, I reminded myself of the master's admonition and made a special effort in looking for an easier word.'[2]

So he began to develop his own simple and direct style which would break down the barrier between the old Chinese-influenced **literati** and the mass of a well-educated but basically Japanese speaking public.

And here I came to the conclusion that I must change the whole style, or concept, of expression in order to reach a wider public. However much **kana** (Japanese syllabary) one might use between the Chinese characters, if the basic style was Chinese, the result would stay difficult. On the contrary, suppose one used the plebeian Japanese for basic style, even when some Chinese characters were mixed in for convenience, it would stay plebeian and easy to read. And so, I mixed the popular Japanese and the graceful Chinese together in one sentence, desecrating the sacred domain of the classical, so to say, but all for the convenience of reaching a wide circle with the new thoughts of the modern civilization.[3]

His freedom to experiment and to avoid over-elaboration was increased by his conscious decision not to show his work to high-brow readers before it was published. 'All of my books were done entirely on my own initiative without orders from or consultation with others. I never showed the manuscripts to any of my friends, to say nothing of asking prominent scholars for prefaces and

---

[1] Fukuzawa, **Collected Works**, 4
[2] Fukuzawa, **Collected Works**, 5
[3] Fukuzawa, **Collected Works**, 6

inscriptions.'¹ On the other hand he did want to make sure that they could be understood by ordinary readers. And so, just as Tocqueville had every word read by his father and brother, Fukuzawa showed his work to ordinary members of the household. 'At that time, I used to tell my friends that I would not be satisfied unless these books could be understood by uneducated farmers and merchants, or even a serving woman just out of the countryside when read to her through the paper door. And so, I did not once show my manuscript to a scholar of Chinese for criticism and correction. Rather, I let women folks and children in my house read it for rewriting those portions which they had difficulty in understanding.'² He believed, correctly, that this attention to simplicity of style was one of the major reasons why his books reached millions of ordinary Japanese readers; 'the style of my writing is generally plain and easy to read. That has been recognized by the public and I too fully believe it is.'³ Nishikawa comments that 'Fukuzawa's style in **An Encouragement of Learning**, and in other textbooks and manuals was completely new in Japan.'⁴

As well as overcoming the much greater gap in vocabulary, Fukuzawa faced problems which were far greater than that of his Enlightenment predecessors. One of these was the intricacy and ambiguity of even the ordinary Japanese language. He gave the following example of its notorious ambiguity. 'Since the first line may signify either 'gourd' or 'warfare', the second has the idea of 'the beginning', and the last may equally be taken for 'cold' or 'rocket', the whole verse may be read in two ways: 1) The first drink from the gourd, we take it cold. 2) The first shot of the war, we do it with the rocket.'⁵

Another difficulty lay at the heart of his enterprise. He was trying to introduce a whole new world from the West, full of alien concepts. Many of these had no Japanese equivalents. He therefore had to invent a new language to deal with such topics as profit, rights of man, and so on. Thinking about this, 'I was led finally to determine that I should make myself a pioneer in creating new words and characters for the Japanese language. Indeed, I created a number of new words. For instance, the English word 'steam' had traditionally been translated **joki**, but I wanted to shorten it.'⁶ In this process he was faced with innumerable difficulties. The very things which he had been most interested in and were distinctively western, small details of everyday life, important institutional features, were the most difficult to translate. 'Therefore, what gave me the most difficulty was the common words which were too common in the native land to call for explanation in a dictionary.'⁷ And it was equally difficult to move out of his Japanese categories to understand what he was to translate. 'Another reminiscence is of 'direct tax' and 'indirect tax' which I came upon in an English book. Direct means 'straight reaching', and with the negating 'in-' it will indicate 'deviating'. So far, quite clear. But then, in taxes how could there be 'straight' and 'deviating' taxes?'⁸

---

¹Fukuzawa, **Autobiography**, 217
²Fukuzawa, **Collected Works**, 6
³Fukuzawa, **Collected Works**, 2
⁴ Nishikawa, 'Fukuzawa', 8
⁵Fukuzawa, **Autobiography**, 146
⁶Fukuzawa, **Collected Works**, 10
⁷Fukuzawa, **Collected Works**, 36
⁸Fukuzawa, **Collected Works**, 37

Given all this, it is not surprising that his translations contain numerous cases where he has shifted the meaning somewhat. Often this was deliberate. In the original account of how the western family worked, Fukuzawa read that the primary relationship was between husband and wife. When he translated this, he deliberately changed this to read so that the primary relationship was between parents and children.[1] Another example is as follows. The original work upon which the 'translation' comes is: "From these few examples, it is perceived that political economy is not an artificial system, but an explanation of the operation of certain natural laws. In explaining this system, the teacher is not more infallible than the teacher of geology or medicine."[2] This was translated as follows: 'Economics is in its essentials clearly not a man-made law. 'Since the purpose of economics is to explain natural laws (**tennen no teisoku**) that arise spontaneously in the world, the explanation of its principles is [to trade or commerce] like making clear the relation of geology to descriptive physical geography or of pathology to medicine."[3] There are several subtle shifts here which change the meaning quite considerably. A great deal could be learnt about Japanese mentality by studying the way Fukuzawa refracted western concepts through the lens of his mind.

As for his actual method of working, his writings contain a few hints. It is clear that he worked at great speed. In one record case 'There was no pausing for the master nor the employees before the thirty-seventh day when all the work was done and several hundred copies of the two volumes of '**Eikoku Gijiin Dan**' were ready. This thirty-seven days from the day the author took up his writing till the publication was a record speed in the days of woodblock printing.'[4] Or again, we are told that 'Fukuzawa Sensei commenced writing 'A Critique of ''The Greater Learning for Women'' and 'The New Greater Learning for Women' last year in the middle of August. Writing one or two or three instalments a day, he finished the whole on September 26...The actual time he spent on the work was some thirty-odd days.'[5] On the other hand his **Outline of a Theory of Civilization** 'took an exceptional amount of time and toil... The manuscripts, which are preserved today, show that they were revised again and again.'[6]

This speed was partly due to the fact that the final writing was often merely putting together thoughts which had occurred to him over a long period and which he had jotted down, like Montesquieu or Tocqueville, mulled over and then turned into prose.

> In his busy schedule, he would, every now and then, take out a copy of **The Greater Learning for Women** by Kaibara Ekken, and for future reference, he would jot down comments in it. Sometimes he would misplace the book and buy a new copy. It is said that there were two or three copies that were lost and replaced, proof that Sensei's interest in the present problem endured over a very long period in time.[7]

---

[1] I owe this example to the kindness of Toshiko Nakamura.
[2] See William and Robert Chambers, (publisher), **Political Economy for Use in Schools, and for Private Instruction** (Edinburgh, 1852), 53-4, actually written by John Hill Burton.
[3] From Craig, 'Fukuzawa', 106, and note 10
[4] Fukuzawa, **Collected Works**, 51
[5] Fukuzawa, **Women**, 170
[6] Nishikawa, 'Fukuzawa', 9
[7] Fukuzawa, **Women**, 171

In fact, much of his work reads more like a conversation between Fukuzawa and his readers. It flows directly out of his life and experiences and is almost autobiographical. In this, again, it is very reminiscent of Tocqueville or Montesquieu's style. Of them, also, it could be written, as it is of Fukuzawa, that 'these thoughts are simply an organized expression of his everyday words and deeds, or a study of his actual life.'[1] Yet, unlike Montesquieu and Adam Smith, it seems to have been important for him to write himself, rather than dictate his work to an amanuensis. It is true that in an illness shortly before his death he did dictate his **Autobiography**, but after that when 'he found some spare time and tried dictating some of his criticisms of **The Greater Learning for Women**...he found that dictation was unfit for the purpose, and he took to seriously writing his views...'[2]

As for his speculations on those deeper problems of logic and causation to which Montesquieu, Smith and Tocqueville devoted so much attention, I have not been able to find anything particularly novel or original in his translated work. He was perfectly familiar with the current logic of scientific and social explanation and as a great admirer of J.S. Mill expounded these ideas to his audience. 'Every action has a cause. We can subdivide this into proximate and remote causes. The proximate are more readily visible than the remote causes. There are more of the former than of the latter. Proximate causes are apt to mislead people by their complexity, whereas remote causes, once discovered, are certain and unchanging. Therefore, the process of tracing a chain of causality is to begin from proximate causes and work back to the remote causes. The farther back the process is traced, the more the number of causes decreases, and several actions can be explained by one cause.'[3] He illustrated this with two examples. In one he showed how by tracing back along links of a chain, the proximate causes of water boiling was burning wood, but if one moved back along further one found oxygen - the same cause that made humans breath.[4]

Likewise as a student of Buckle and others he was perfectly familiar with the idea of the statistical tendencies which lie behind everyday life, made famous later in Durkheim's study of suicide. 'If we chart the figures for land area and population, the prices of commodities and wage rates, and the number of the married, the living, the sick, and those who die, the general conditions of a society will become clear at a glance, even things one ordinarily cannot calculate. For example, I have read that the number of marriages in England every year follows fluctuations in the price of grain. When grain prices go up, marriages decline, and vice versa. The ratio can be predicted...' Thus, while the proximate cause of marriage 'were the desires of the couple, the wishes of their parents, the advice of the matchmaker, and so forth' these were not 'sufficient to explain the matter'. 'Only when we go beyond them to look for the remote cause, and come up with the factor of the price of rice, do we unerringly obtain the real cause

---

[1] Fukuzawa, **Women**, 172
[2] Fukuzawa, **Women**, 171
[3] Fukuzawa, **Civilization**, 53
[4] Fukuzawa, **Civilization**, 52-3

controlling the frequency of marriages in the country'.[1] He was thus competent in a wide area of sociological and scientific method.

[1] Fukuzawa, **Civilization**, 52-3

9. THE CIVILIZING PROCESS

In order to see where Japan fitted into the scheme of things and how it could develop further into a higher 'civilization', Fukuzawa made use of a 'stage theory' of progress. He believed that 'civilization is not a dead thing; it is something vital and moving.' Therefore 'it must pass through sequences and stages; primitive people advance to semi-developed forms, the semi-developed advance to civilization, and civilization itself is even now in the process of advancing forward.' He reminded his readers that 'Europe also had to pass through these phases in its evolution to its present level.'[1] His 'stages' of civilization are very similar to those of Adam Smith, Kames, Ferguson and other Scottish Enlightenment thinkers, which then became absorbed as the foundations for anthropology in the following century.

We are told that 'As early as 1869 Fukuzawa had described humanity as divided into four 'kinds'. Of the lowest kind, **konton**, the aborigines of Australia and New Guinea were examples; the second lowest kind, **banya**, was represented by the nomads of Mongolia and Arabia; the third lowest, **mikai**, by the peoples of Asiatic countries such as China, Turkey and Persia; while the highest kind, **kaika-bummei**, was exemplified by western nations such as America, England, France and Germany.'[2] This, of course, more or less exactly parallels the normal anthropological division into hunter-gatherers, tribesmen, peasants and urban-industrial societies, although they would replace value-laden words like 'lower' and 'higher'.

A few years later he tried a three-fold model. We are told that he 'had already read the stage theory in J.H.Burton's **Political Economy**, pp.6-7, in which three stages are called 'barbarous and/or primitive', 'half civilized' and 'civilized'.'[3] In 1876 he distinguished between **Yaban** - illiterate savages; **Hankai** - peoples such as Chinese and Japanese 'who, though they might possess flourishing literatures, yet had no curiosity about the natural world, no original ideas for inventing new things, and no ability to criticize and improve on accepted customs and conveniences; and **Bummei** - civilized people who had all these qualities.'[4] Or again, he wrote that 'present-day China has to be called semi-developed in comparison with Western countries. But if we compare China with countries of South Africa, or, to take an example more at hand, if we compare the Japanese people with the Ezo [Ainu] then both China and Japan can be called civilized.'[5] These 'stage' models, so popular after Darwin, were combined with a view of the inevitable **progress** from one to another which is another of the features which he shared with many European thinkers.

Carmen Blacker describes his general belief in the inevitability of progress as follows. 'Simply, Fukuzawa believed, because progress was a 'natural law'. Man's nature was such that he was bound and destined to progress, and hence would naturally, even unconsciously, fulfil the conditions which would lead to

---

[1] Fukuzawa, **Civilization**, 15
[2] Blacker, **Fukuzawa**, 146, note 15
[3] Nishikawa, 'Fukuzawa', 17, note 26
[4] Blacker, **Fukuzawa**, 146, note 15
[5] Fukuzawa, **Civilization**, 14

progress. The process could, certainly, be arrested artificially for a certain time, but ultimately it would prove to be like a tide which would sweep all obstacles out of its way.'[1] Hence his reference, as we have seen, to the surge of individual rights and liberty. And hence his belief in the inevitability of growing freedom. He followed Tocqueville in believing that "Careful study of politics will show us that there is an unceasing force causing autocracy to change to freedom, just as water always flows towards the low ground. There may certainly be reversals of this tendency, but they are only temporary fluctuations. The facts show indisputably that the long-term trend stretching over tens of thousands of years is for monarchy to give way to democracy, and for tyranny to give way to liberalism."[2] Like Tocqueville, he had visited America and seen the future - and there could be little doubt in his mind that the future lay in wealth, equality and liberty.

Hence his interest in those historians in the west who most fully endorsed the strong 'whig' view of history, the march of civilization and progress. We are told that 'Buckle's **History of Civilization in England** and Guizot's **General History of Civilization in England** were examples of the supremely optimistic school of positivist historical writing which grew up in Western Europe during the second half of the nineteenth century...Both...were translated early into Japanese and became the guiding scriptures of the **Keimo** school of historiography known as **bummeishiron** (history of civilization)...'[3]

Despite the belief that history was, in the long term, on his side, Fukuzawa recognized that there could be hiccups - like the 250 years of Tokugawa rule. He also had periods of doubt. As Albert Craig argues, we can detect three main phases in his thought. During the 1860's and first half of the 1870's he believed that rapid progress was possible. Then the 'year 1875 is a transitional point in Fukuzawa's thought. He has become uncertain. He has become a moderate relativist. Utopian civilization has receded several thousand years into the future.'[4] After some twenty years or so of doubt, he returned to his greater optimism and 'In some respects this was a revival of Fukuzawa's earlier 'enlightenment' belief in a beneficent natural order, for once again he saw progress toward an ideal society as possible within a finite period of time.'[5] The period from roughly 1875 to 1895 exactly coincides with the nationalistic and aggressive phase of his thought.

Yet whether the highest level of civilization was close or far, Fukuzawa's main task was to analyze its constituent elements and to understand how a country like Japan could adopt it. This took him to his deepest analysis of what was special about the West. Having located the mystery roughly in the area of liberty and equality, he was still faced with the problems of the institutional mechanisms needed to encourage these nebulous virtues. It was not a simple matter of setting up schools, newspapers, universities and so on. All this would help, but there was a deeper essence to be grasped. In attempting to penetrate to

---

[1] Blacker, **Fukuzawa**, 98-9
[2] Blacker, **Fukuzawa**, 112
[3] Blacker, Fukuzawa, 92-3
[4] Craig, 'Fukuzawa', 124
[5] Craig, 'Fukuzawa, 137

the 'spirit' of the West, Fukuzawa provides a number of insightful passages on the mystery of the unusual civilization which he saw and read about on his trip to America and Europe.

10. THE SEPARATION OF SPHERES

Fukuzawa based his ideas on the work of Guizot and Mill. This led him to believe, like Montesquieu, that there must be a separation and balance of powers. If there was the Confucian fusion of kinship and politics, there would be hierarchical absolutism. If there was a fusion of politics and religion, there would be despotism. For instance, he commented that in the case of Buddhism, 'its teaching has been entirely absorbed by political authority. What shines throughout the world is not the radiance of Buddha's teachings but the glory of Buddhism's political authority. Hence it is not surprising that there is no independent religious structure within the Buddhist religion.'[1] Or again, if there was a fusion of society and economy there would be stagnation. If there was a fusion of public life and private morality there would be absolutism. The parts needed to be separated and artificially held apart.

Let us look first at a few of his general remarks on the necessity for a dynamic balance, a tense contradiction or separation between spheres. 'To use a simile, if you take metals such as gold, silver, copper and iron, and melt them together, you would not end up with gold, or silver, or copper, or iron, but with a compound mixture that preserves a certain balance between the various elements, and in which each adds strength to the others. This is how Western civilization is.'[2] There must be a never-ending contest, which no part wins.

> The point of difference between Western and other civilizations is that Western society does not have a uniformity of opinions; various opinions exist side by side without fusing into one. For example, there are theories which advocate governmental authority; others argue for the primacy of religious authority. There are proponents of monarchy, theocracy, aristocracy, and democracy. Each goes its own way, each maintains its own position. Although they vie with one another, no single one of them ever completely wins out. Since the contest never is decided, all sides grudgingly are forced to live with the others.[3]

The general openness of the society can only be guaranteed if freedom to dominate is held in check. 'Now in the first place, the freedom of civilization cannot be bought at the expense of some other freedom. It can only exist by not infringing upon other rights and privileges, other opinions and powers, all of which should exist in some balance. It is only possible for freedom to exist when freedom is restricted.'[4] Again we have the idea of the dynamic balance of powers and opinions. Many opinions and many institutions should flourish in healthy competition; this is the essence and secret of western civilization.

> Once they start living side by side, despite their mutual hostility, they each recognize the others' rights and allow them to go their ways. Since no view is able to monopolize the whole situation and must allow the other schools of thought room to function, each makes its own contribution to one area of civilization by being true to its own position, until finally, taken together, the end result is one civilization. This is how autonomy and freedom have developed in the West.'[5]

---

[1] Fukuzawa, **Civilization**, 147
[2] Fukuzawa, **Civilization**, 135
[3] Fukuzawa, **Civilization**, 125
[4] Fukuzawa, **Civilization**, 135
[5] Fukuzawa, **Civilization**, 125

The domination of one sphere, for instance the kinship or political system, is a 'disease'. 'All of this is the result of the imbalance of power, an evil that has arisen from not paying attention to the second step of things. If we do not take cognizance of this evil and get rid of the disease of imbalance, whether the country is at peace or in turmoil no real progress will be made in the level of civilization of the country.'[1]

A particular danger, of course, was for the imbalance to lead to the growth of central political power, political absolutism. 'This I call the curse of imbalance. Those in power must always take stock of themselves.'[2] There must be limits on the powerful. 'Thus, in any area of human affairs, whether it be the government, the people, scholars, or bureaucrats, when there is one who has power, whether it be intellectual or physical, there must be a limit to that power.'[3] As Carmen Blacker summarizes his thought here, 'The reason why it was so important for the government's and people's respective spheres to be kept separate was that in the proper balance between the two lay one of the secrets of progress in civilization.' Thus 'It was precisely in her failure to appreciate the importance of this balance, Fukuzawa was convinced, that Japan's greatest weakness lay.'[4] He argued that the government should be strictly limited in its objectives. Like the 'nightwatchman state' advocated by his Scottish Enlightenment predecessors a hundred years earlier, he believed that the view that the 'government should not encroach on the private sphere meant that it should have nothing to do with such activities as religion, schools, agriculture or commerce...'[5]

In advocating this balance and separation, he realized that he was going against the grain of the Confucian and Chinese legacy in Japan. There was the strong inclination we have already seen to merge kinship and political allegiance which tended towards autocracy in both. 'In the countries of Asia, the ruler has been called the parent of the people, the people have been called his subjects and children. In China, the work of the government has been called the office of shepherd of the masses, and local officials were called the shepherds of such-and-such provinces.'[6] It permeated the whole of the hierarchical structure of deference and arrogance which he had noted in his youth.

> While bowing before one man, he was lording it over another. For example, if there were ten people in A,B,C, order, B in his relation to A expressed subservience and humility, to a point where the humiliation he suffered ought to have been intolerable. But in his relation with C he was able to be regally high-handed. Thus his humiliation in the former case was made up for by the gratification he derived from the latter. Any dissatisfaction evened itself out. C took compensation from D, D demanded the same from E, and so on down the line. It was like dunning the neighbour on one's east for the sum loaned to the neighbour on one's west.[7]

It was thus a disease of imbalance which permeated all relations, not just governmental power but also all social relations. 'According to the above argument, arbitrary use of authority and imbalance of power is not found in the

---

[1] Fukuzawa, **Civilization**, 160
[2] Fukuzawa, **Civilization**, 135
[3] Fukuzawa, **Civilization**, 135
[4] Blacker, **Fukuzawa**, 110
[5] Blacker, **Fukuzawa**, 108
[6] Fukuzawa, **Learning**, 70
[7] Fukuzawa, **Civilization**, 155

government alone. It is embedded in the spirit of the Japanese people as a whole. This spirit is a conspicuous dividing line between the Western world and Japan, and though we must now turn to seeking its causes, we are faced with an extremely difficult task.'[1]

Japan did have one great advantage over China, however. This was that the crucial separation between ritual and political power had occurred many centuries earlier when the Shogun became the **de facto** political ruler, while the Emperor was the ritual head. Fukuzawa saw this separation, the breaking of what in the West was the tendency towards Caesaro-Papist absolutism, as a point at which freedom could enter. Whereas in China to attempt to challenge any part of the social or intellectual system was simultaneously to commit heresy, treason and filial impiety, in Japan reason could find a chink between the opposing concept of ritual and political power.

Fukuzawa expounded his interesting thoughts on this matter at some length.

> The two concepts of the most sacrosanct and the powerful were so obviously distinct that people could hold in their heads, as it were, the simultaneous existence and functioning of the two ideas. Once they did so, they could not help adding a third, the principle of reason. With the principle of reason added to the idea of reverence for the imperial dignity and the idea of military rule, none of these three concepts was able to predominate. And since no single concept predominated, there naturally followed a spirit of freedom.'[2]

'It was truly Japan's great good fortune that the ideas of the most sacrosanct and of the most powerful balanced each other in such a way as to allow room between them for some exercise of intelligence and the play of reason.'[3]

Japan's good fortune could be seen by comparing its situation with that in China, where the normal **ancien regime** blending of religious and political power was at its most extreme with the ancient rule of its God-Emperor. The situation in Japan 'obviously was not the same as in China, where the people looked up to one completely autocratic ruler and with single-minded devotion were slaves to the idea that the most sacrosanct and the most powerful were embodied in the same person. In the realm of political thought, therefore, the Chinese were impoverished and the Japanese were rich.'[4]

Another fusion is between the economy and the society. Anthropologists have written a good deal about how the economy is 'embedded' in the society, that is to say it is impossible to separate economic and social transactions in the majority of societies. Polanyi believed that the 'great transformation' from this situation occurred in eighteenth century England with the rise of commercial capitalism.[5] Max Weber and Karl Marx believed it occurred in the fifteenth and sixteenth centuries with the rise of capitalism and the separation of the social and economic.[6] Fukuzawa's **Autobiography** provides a delightful instance of an attempt to 'disembed' an economy, as an individual and at a theoretical level.

---

[1] Fukuzawa, **Civilization**, 138
[2] Fukuzawa, **Civilization**, 21-2
[3] Fukuzawa, **Civilizations**, 22
[4] Fukuzawa, **Civilization**, 22
[5] Polanyi, **Great Transformation**
[6] See Macfarlane, **Individualism**, ch.2, for a summary of their views.

As a member of a Samurai family, Fukuzawa's **bushi-do** ethic was strongly opposed to purely commercial transactions. This took the form, for instance, of fearing money - that ultimate symbol of the market place. He described how there were embarrassing altercations with merchants, who refused to receive payment for their goods, presumably preferring social rewards. 'He wanted to give the money back to me, but I insisted on leaving it, because I remembered what my mother had told me. After some arguing, which was almost like quarrelling, I forced the money on the merchant and came home.'[1] Fukuzawa admitted that 'When I went to Osaka and became a student at Ogata school, I was still afraid of money.'[2] He remembered that 'I had no taste or inclination to engage in buying or selling, lending or borrowing. Also the old idea of the samurai that trade was not our proper occupation prevailed in my mind, I suppose.'[3] Thus he organized his life so that 'Our home is like a world apart; the new methods of Western civilization do not enter our household finances.'[4] From this personal experience of the power, alienation and aggressiveness of capitalist, money, transactions, Fukuzawa gained the insight to be able to begin to bridge the gap between the competitive western capitalism he had seen in America, and the embedded world around him.

A key incident was when Fukuzawa started to read the educational course published by William and Robert Chambers. There was a volume explaining in a simple way the principles of western economics. Fukuzawa described how 'I was reading Chamber's book on economics. When I spoke of the book to a certain high official in the treasury bureau one day, he became much interested and wanted me to show him a translation.'[5] So Fukuzawa began to translate the work into Japanese, a translation which formed a part of the second volume of his **Conditions of the West**. As he did so he ran into an illuminating difficulty in translating the central premise of western economic systems. 'I began translating it (it comprised some twenty chapters) when I came upon the word 'competition' for which there was no equivalent in Japanese, and I was obliged to use an invention of my own, **kyoso**, literally, 'race-fight'. When the official saw my translation, he appeared much impressed. Then he said suddenly, 'Here is the word 'fight'. What does it mean? It is such an unpeaceful word."[6] The confrontation between the war of all against all, competitive individualistic behaviour in the market-place, and the Confucian ethic of harmony and co-operation has seldom been more graphically exposed.[7]

It was now necessary for Fukuzawa to defend and explain his translation. "That is nothing new', I replied 'That is exactly what all Japanese merchants are doing. For instance, if one merchant begins to sell things cheap, his neighbour will try to sell them even cheaper. Or if one merchant improves his merchandise to attract more buyers, another will try to take the trade from him by offering goods of still better quality. Thus all merchants 'race and fight' and this is the

---
[1] Fukuzawa, **Autobiography**, 262
[2] Fukuzawa, **Autobiography**, 263
[3] Fukuzawa, **Autobiography**, 281
[4] Fukuzawa, **Autobiography**, 285
[5] Fukuzawa, **Autobiography**, 190
[6] Fukuzawa, **Autobiography**, 190
[7] As Koestler, **Lotus**, 221, for instance, noted

way money values are fixed. This process is termed **kyoso** in the science of economics."¹ All this was half-true, as he knew. But he was also aware of a basic difference between Japan and the West, and had to insist that the bitter confrontational element in western capitalism had to be swallowed, not merely by merchants, but by everyone. 'I suppose he would rather have seen some such phrase as 'men being kind to each other' in a book on economics, or a man's loyalty to his lord, open generosity from a merchant in times of national stress, etc. But I said to him, 'If you do not agree to the word 'fight', I am afraid I shall have to erase it entirely. There is no other term that is faithful to the original.'"²

Fukuzawa noticed a strange paradox, which had also intrigued his Enlightenment predecessors. While western society was driven by narrow, anti-social and, it would seem, self-interested greed, the result was public wealth and a high standard of honesty and private morality. While his Japanese Confucian contemporaries subscribed to a benevolent Confucian desire to promote harmony and kindness, the product was dishonesty and private immorality. He summarized the difference very elegantly. 'Westerners try to expand their business to gain greater profits in the long run. Because they are afraid dishonest dealings will jeopardize long-range profits, they have to be honest. This sincerity does not come from the heart, but from the wallet. To put the same idea in other words, Japanese are greedy on a small scale, foreigners are greedy on a large scale.'³ While Japanese merchants, like Chinese ones, could not be trusted 'Western merchants, in contrast, are exact and honest in their business dealings. They show a small sample of woven goods, someone buys several thousand times as much of the material, and what is delivered differs in no wise from the sample. The buyer receives the shipment with his mind at peace; he does not even open any of the boxes to check the contents.'⁴ It was a strange paradox. Fukuzawa noted that growing affluence seemed to lead to an improvement in private morals. 'In England, France and other countries in the modern world, the people of the middle class progressively amassed wealth; with it they also elevated their own moral conduct.'⁵

What Fukuzawa realized was that in order to increase 'rationality' in economic transactions, such exchanges needed to be separated from the social relationship, just as in order to achieve 'rational' social relations, one had to separate politics and kinship. He also realized that in order to achieve 'rational' science, one had to accept the separation of fact and value, of humanity and nature, of the moral and the physical. This was especially difficult in a neo-Confucian society where the very essence of the system was to blend the human and natural worlds. We are told that Japanese Confucianists 'thought that western science explained everything by physical laws: This was treating nature as dead and mechanical, unrelated to man, and hence destroying the harmony of the universe.'⁶ Fukuzawa was indeed taking on a difficult task.

---

¹Fukuzawa, **Autobiography**, 190
²Fukuzawa, **Autobiography**, 191
³Fukuzawa, **Civilization**, 123
⁴Fukuzawa, **Civilization**, 122
⁵Fukuzawa, **Civilization**, 145
⁶Blacker, **Fukuzawa**, 49; cf 87

11. LIBERTY AND EQUALITY

As we have seen, Fukuzawa was born into a system which made strenuous efforts to inhibit individual 'selfishness'. The basic element of Japanese social structure at Fukuzawa's level was not the individual, but the clan, the 'house'. He described how 'The Japanese people suffered for many years under the yoke of despotism. Lineage was the basis of power. Even intelligent men were entirely dependent upon houses of high lineage. The whole age was, as it were, under the thumb of lineage. Throughout the land there was no room for human initiative; everything was in a condition of stagnation.'[1] Putting it another way, he described how 'The millions of Japanese at that time were closed up inside millions of individual boxes. They were separated from one another by walls with little room to move around.'[2] In Japan when 'we deal with a person, be he rich or poor, strong or weak, wise or ignorant, capable or incompetent, we either fear him or look down upon him, entirely on the basis of his social position. A spirit of independence has never existed in even the slightest degree.' This feature came out especially when set against what he had seen in America and Europe. 'If we compare the Western attitude of independence with that of us insulated Japanese, we can see how enormous the difference is.'[3]

His reading of Guizot, J. S. Mill and others made him conclude that the differences were of long standing. The individuality and freedom in the west seemed to be rooted in the period of turmoil after the fall of Rome when 'the German barbarians left behind a legacy of autonomy and freedom'.[4] If this were the case one might have expected that 'the Japanese warrior class would also produce its own spirit of independence and autonomy'.[5] Yet, as a member of that class, he knew that this was not so. For 'although the samurai of this time seemed fiercely independent, their spirit sprang neither from a personal, chauvinistic attitude nor from a strong individuality that exulted in the self's freedom from all outside influences. It was always motivated by something outside the person, or at least aided by it.'[6] Thus he argued that 'human relations in Asia have evolved into definite patterns of discrimination and prejudice, and social feelings are lukewarm. As if this were not bad enough, despotic government has also made possible the enactment of laws that prohibit political factions and public discussions.'[7] Much of Fukuzawa's work was concerned with liberating himself and the Japanese people from these fetters, for he believed that 'There are no innate bonds around men. They are born free and unrestricted, and become free adult men and women.'[8]

As a disciple of Mill, and hence in the tradition of Montesquieu and Tocqueville, Fukuzawa advocated private liberty, that right to be free from external pressures which is central to western thought. He argued that 'each man deserves his private liberty. It is not proper, and society does not permit

---

[1] Fukuzawa, **Civilization**, 65
[2] Fukuzawa, **Civilization**, 160
[3] Fukuzawa, **Civilization**, 161
[4] Fukuzawa, **Civilization**, 153
[5] Fukuzawa, **Civilization**, 153
[6] Fukuzawa, **Civilization**, 153
[7] Fukuzawa, **Civilization**, 73
[8] Fukuzawa, **Learning**, 3

prying into the privacy of an independent man.'[1] And when he said 'man', he was speaking of mankind and not the male gender. He set out his views of the meaning of freedom, directly following Mill, in the following words. A person 'can conduct himself in freedom, as long as he does not infringe upon the rights of others. He can go as he pleases, work or play, engage in some business, study hard or, if that does not agree with him, loaf around the whole day long. Provided these actions do not affect others, there is no reason for men to censure them from the sidelines.'[2]

Like all those who have thought deeply about the matter, Fukuzawa realized that the other side of the coin of liberty was equality; one was not possible without a certain amount of the other. The link between the two can be seen, for example, in the contextual instability of language and behaviour which he noted. In an interesting passage he compared the fixity of the western social structure to the contextual situation in Japan, which was dependent on the power relationship.

> 'Comparing these social patterns to material objects, power in the West is like iron; it does not readily expand or contract. On the other hand, the power of the Japanese warriors was as flexible as rubber, adapting itself to whatever it came in contact with. In contact with inferiors, it swelled up immensely; in contact with those above, it shrivelled up and shrank. The sum total of this hierarchy of power constituted that whole known as the prestige of the military houses...'[3]

He had found a very different world in America and Europe. He found that 'even in the West not everyone is equal in terms of wealth or prestige. The strong and wealthy often control the weak and poor in a cruel and arrogant manner. The weak and poor, in turn, may fawn on and deceive others. The ugly aspects of human life are certainly no different from what we find among Japanese. Sometimes they are even worse.'[4] Yet the situation, though on the surface just as bad, was different. For 'even with such social injustice there is still a pervading spirit of individuality and nothing hinders the expansion of the human spirit. Cruelty and arrogance are merely by-products of wealth and power; flattery and deception are merely by-products of poverty and weakness. Neither might nor weakness is innate; they can be dealt with by means of human intelligence.'[5]

His distinction between the **de jure** and the **de facto** helped him to explain that changing the laws was only part of the solution. He noted optimistically that 'In one powerful stroke the great upheaval of the Imperial Restoration abolished the class system. Since then, we have enjoyed a society of equality for all peoples: the daimyo, courtiers, samurai, farmers, artisans, and merchants - all became of equal rank and marriages became possible among them. And so, a great man is now able to openly marry the daughter of a petty merchant or a soil-tilling farmer.'[6] Yet the spirit of subservience, the actual attitudes, were slower to change. 'Since the Meiji Restoration, the equality of all peoples has been declared. Farmers and merchants are supposed to be enjoying this privilege, but

---

[1] Fukuzawa, **Women**, 101
[2] Fukuzawa, **Learning**, 50
[3] Fukuzawa, **Civilization**, 155
[4] Fukuzawa, **Civilization**, 160-1
[5] Fukuzawa, **Civilization**, 161
[6] Fukuzawa, **Women**, 81-2

they are still as subservient as ever, so difficult is it to break away from old ways.'[1]

Thus Fukuzawa explicitly set out in his writing and in his life to challenge the premise of the basic inequality of man. In order to test the inherited system of deference and how much of it was built into the symbolism of gestures and speech, he carried out an experiment as he walked down a high road. 'So I proceeded, accosting everyone who came along. Without any allowance for their appearance, I spoke alternately, now in samurai fashion, now merchant like. In every instance, for about seven miles on my way, I saw that people would respond according to the manner in which they were addressed - with awe or with indifference.'[2] But even Fukuzawa found limits to his egalitarian spirit. 'I have always used the honorific form of address in my speech generally - not of course to the lowly workmen or grooms or petty merchants in the really casual order of life, but to all other persons including the young students and the children in my household.'[3]

His attack on the premise of inequality, we are told, 'contradicted one of the most fundamental assumptions of the traditional political philosophy. Hitherto it had been commonly believed, not that men were naturally equal, but that society was naturally hierarchical.'[4] Fukuzawa proclaimed the opposite.

Although a poor peasant and a high daimyo 'differ like the clouds above and the mud below, still from the point of view of inherent human rights all men are equal without the least distinction between superior and inferior human beings.'[5] In the very first sentence of his **Advancement of Learning** he made the revolutionary proclamation, like Rousseau, of the natural equality of men. 'It is said that heaven does not create one man above or below another man. This means that when men are born from heaven they are all equal.'[6] He then explained how 'At the beginning of the first section I said that all men are equal, and that they can live in freedom and independence without hereditary status distinctions. I want to develop that idea further here.'[7] He did this by explaining the difference between inherent, **de jure** equality, and achieved, **de facto**, inequality. 'Therefore, if we inquire into the balance of human relations, we must say that all men are equal. They may not be equal in outward appearances. Equality means equality in essential human rights.'[8] It was really only relative wealth that gave temporary advantage, not birth or occupation. "Since we are poor we obey the rich, but only as long as we are poor must we submit to them. Our submission will disappear along with our poverty, while their control over us will vanish along with their riches."[9]

---

[1] Fukuzawa, **Women**, 30
[2] Fukuzawa, **Autobiography**, 245
[3] Fukuzawa, **Autobiography**, 193
[4] Blacker, **Fukuzawa**, 101
[5] Fukuzawa, **Learning**, 10
[6] Fukuzawa, **Learning**, 1
[7] Fukuzawa, **Learning**, 10
[8] Fukuzawa, **Learning**, 10
[9] Fukuzawa, **Civilization**, 161

The ideas here were so revolutionary that there was no word for them in Japanese. 'For example, the one principle which was basic to Fukuzawa's entire philosophy was **dokuritsu-jison**, a compound word which he coined. Though other English translations have been made of this, perhaps the best translation is "independence and self-respect."[1] We are told that 'To a nineteenth-century Japanese, on the other hand, **dokuritsu-jison** was a shockingly revolutionary Western concept designed to undermine the entire Confucian social order which for many centuries had welded Japanese society into a rigidly-stratified yet cohesive unit.'[2]

---

[1] Fukuzawa, **Speeches**, 72
[2] Fukuzawa, **Speeches**, 72

12. FAMILY RELATIONS

Fukuzawa's ideas were particularly revolutionary when they were applied to the Japanese family and especially the relations between men and women. One of Fukuzawa's central interests throughout his life was in the practical effects of equality on the relations of men and women. he realized that gender relations both mirrored and contributed to other forms of social relations. He may have developed both his interest in the subject and his advanced view partly from his own unusual mother, whose independence of mind and egalitarian outlook we encountered in an earlier chapter. That influence may help to explain how he developed such an early interest in the subject, and why it continued literally until his death-bed. We are told that 'Fukuzawa's thoughts on women date back to the days when he first came to Tokyo at the age of twenty-five and was already jotting his critical comments in the margins of his copy of **The Greater Learning for Women**. Toward his end, when he slipped into a coma following a stroke that was to eventually take his life, he was heard mumbling about women's rights.'[1]

This early interest was greatly reinforced by his three visits to the West. To his surprise he found that 'It appears that in the civilized countries of the West, much of the social intercourse is managed by women, and even though they do not run society, they work in harmony among men, and help smooth the situation.'[2] In particular, in America, he thought 'women are high, men are humble.'[3] By Asian standards, indeed, they seemed too free and equal. 'For instance, from the standards of Chinese ethics, the behaviour of Western ladies and gentlemen is barbarous, with no sense of etiquette or propriety, because they talk together, laugh together, and, though they do not go so far as to bathe together, they sit and eat together, and they pass things to each other directly from hand to hand; not only that, they hold hands - and among themselves that is considered good manners.'[4] Indeed even Fukuzawa was a little shocked by the extremes. 'In the West, women's behaviour sometimes goes beyond control; they make light of men; their minds are sharp, but their thoughts may be tarnished and their personal behaviour unchaste; they may neglect their own homes and flutter about society like butterflies. Such behaviour is no model for Japanese women.'[5]

As well as personal observation, Fukuzawa learnt about the dynamics of egalitarian family life from his reading, including the work of J.S. Mill. For example his reading of works on domestic relations in Chambers' **Educational Course** suggests a model of the companionate, affectionate, western family. This he described for his Japanese readers thus.

> Husband and wife, parents and children in one household constitute a family. Family relationships are bound by feeling. There is no fixed ownership of things, no rules for giving and taking. Things lost are not cried over; things gained are no special cause for jubilation.

---

[1] Fukuzawa, **Women**, x
[2] Fukuzawa, **Women**, 117
[3] Fukuzawa, **Autobiography**, 114
[4] Fukuzawa, **Women**, 177; the reference to bathing together was obviously an allusion to the widespread custom of men and women bathing in the same public bath or hot spring in Japan.
[5] Fukuzawa, **Women**, 35

> Informality is not upbraided, ineptitude does not cause embarrassment. The contentment of the wife or children becomes the joy of the husband or the parents, and the suffering of the husband and parents pains the wife and children too.'[1]

He described how he tried to put this into practice. 'Above all, I believe in love and love only for the relation between parents and children. Even after children are grown, I see no reason for any formality in the relationship. In this my wife and I are perfectly of the same opinion.'[2] Thus he had a strong model of what 'civilized' family life was like and he worked hard to fulfil his wish, which was 'to let the women of Japan grow to be like the women of the West as a first step in their progress.'[3]

In essence, he believed in the innate equality of the genders. 'It is an irrefutable fact that men and women do not differ in their body structures and in the workings of their minds, and that they are equal beings.'[4] This led him to advocate the equal treatment of boy and girl children. 'When a baby girl is born, love her and care for her as much as one would a baby boy; never slacken in vigilance over her because she is a girl. When she grows up, see to her healthy development, first in body and then in mind. In her schooling and other education never discriminate because of her sex.'[5] It also led him to advocate equality in the marriage relationship. 'Not only should women be allowed to share the management of material property, but the affairs of the heart too, whether they are private or public. If a couple always talks things over thoroughly and seriously, then even at the misfortune of the husband's dying early, the household management will not fall entirely into darkness.'[6]

These views were truly revolutionary in late nineteenth century Japan. How unusual they were and how hard Fukuzawa felt he had to work, as well as an impression of his righteous indignation, comes out when we consider his description of the actual position of many Japanese women in his society, set against the ideal model of his hopes and experiences in the West.

Japanese women were without independence. 'They are given no responsibility at all. As in the saying 'Women have no home of their own anywhere in the world,' when she is born, she is brought up in the house which is her father's; when she is grown and married, she lives in a house which is her husband's; when she is old and is being cared for by her son, the house will be her son's. All the family property is her husband's property; women are only allowed to share in the benefits of that property.'[7] In summary, 'Women of our country have no responsibility either inside or outside their homes and their position is very low.'[8] They existed for men. 'In other words, women exist at the mercy of men and their security and their fate are in the hands of men.'[9] Their life was a continuous waiting on men. 'Women's lives are nothing but series of

---

[1] Fukuzawa, **Civilization**, 116
[2] Fukuzawa, **Autobiography**, 304
[3] Fukuzawa, **Women**, 14
[4] Fukuzawa, **Women**, 39
[5] Fukuzawa, **Women**, 61
[6] Fukuzawa, **Women**, 60
[7] Fukuzawa, **Women**, 9
[8] Fukuzawa, **Women**, 11
[9] Fukuzawa, **Women**, 11

services, first to parents when young, then to husbands and parents-in-law when married, and when children come, they are busy caring for them and supervising the food and kitchen work.'[1] They were trapped. 'This is the actual condition of our society, and women are being forced into a narrower and narrower confinement, their sphere of social intercourse made smaller and smaller until they are like birds in a cage.'[2]

Fukuzawa quoted the criticism which outsiders, and particularly American women, made of the situation. Quoting one such visitor, he wrote "The Japanese women are miserable, their lives are truly not worth living, I am sorry for them. I pity them. We Americans would not tolerate such a situation for even a moment. We would fight even at the risk of our lives. Japan and America are separate countries, but the women of both are sisters of the same human species. We American women must do something to destroy this evil custom.' She said this with tears falling and she gritted her teeth.'[3] He clearly felt sympathy for such criticism, noting that 'when the truth becomes known and the ladies of the West see the actual conditions with their own eyes, they are liable to condemn Japan as a hell and inferno for women.'[4]

Given the huge gap between the actual situation as he perceived it, and the ideal 'civilized' state of equality which he hoped to achieve, how was Fukuzawa to proceed? The first thing he did was to put forward an explanation for the low and subservient position of women.

He put forward two major theories to account for the situation. One placed the blame in the medieval period or earlier, where a combination of the feudal political order and the powerful lineage system built up the structural inequality of women. In relation to politics, he wrote that 'In the feudal ages of the past, the whole social system from the government to every aspect of human life was constructed on the idea of authority and compulsion. The relation between men and women naturally also followed this general trend, and men acted like lords and women like vassals.'[5] This political system, Fukuzawa argued, was linked closely to the presence of powerful kinship groups or lineages, which traced descent through the male line and kept property in the hands of men. 'The old custom of the feudal days which valued lineage of a family above all other things and forced the maintenance of the line on the male members of the family, pushing women into a position of virtual non-existence - that custom, from now on, must be discontinued completely.'[6] The idea of male descent must be rejected. Although 'the strange fact is that since very old times in our society, there has been what is called a family, which has been carried on by male descendants.'[7]

In particular, the exclusive rights of men to lineage property must be surrendered. The present situation, he thought, was that 'No women in Japan

---

[1] Fukuzawa, **Women**, 18
[2] Fukuzawa, **Women**, 157
[3] Fukuzawa, **Women**, 199-200
[4] Fukuzawa, **Women**, 57
[5] Fukuzawa, **Women**, 218
[6] Fukuzawa, **Women**, 53-4
[7] Fukuzawa, **Women**, 51

possess any property. As the saying goes, a woman has no house of her own anywhere in this world; thus it is a natural consequence that there is no woman with her own property.'[1] Indeed, the absence of 'property', or rights in assets, extended far beyond physical things like a house. 'At home, she owns no property of her own, and in society she cannot hope for a position of any consequence. The house she lives in is a man's house and the children she brings up are her husband's children.'[2] All this must be changed by completely abandoning the lineage system which had existed for hundreds of years, and moving towards the European and American conjugal family model.

Fukuzawa added a second argument, not entirely consistent with his first, which placed most of the blame on Chinese, and particularly neo-Confucianist ideology. In this theory, he played down the feudal and lineage arguments and stressed that Japanese women's position had declined dramatically during the period from the seventeenth century. 'In my own thoughts, I suspect that the restrictions on women's behaviour is something that began in the prolonged peace of the Tokugawa period. When all the armed conflicts in the country ended and the society became settled in the years of Genna [1615-23], Confucianism gradually rose to advocate what it called the great doctrine to clarify the social ranks of high and low, noble and mean.'[3] Or again, he wrote that 'Since the years of Genna [1615-19], when the peace began, most of the samurai youth were brought up under the influence of this Confucianism and its teachings of benevolence, loyalty, etiquette, wisdom, filial piety, brotherly love, loyalty to the master and faithfulness to friends.'[4]

Much of Fukuzawa's work on women is therefore devoted to undoing what he considers to be the harmful effects of neo-Confucian thought, and particularly that work **The Greater Learning for Women** on which he started scribbling critical comments from the age of twenty-five. He described how 'Confucianism characterizes men as **yang** (positive) and women **yin** (negative); that is, men are like the heavens and the sun, and women like the earth and the moon. In other words, one is high and the other is humble, and there are many men who take this idea as the absolute rule of nature. But this **yin-yang** theory is the fantasy of the Confucianists and has no proof or logic.'[5] He wrote with sarcasm how 'In a book called **Onna daigaku** there is enunciated a principle of 'triple obedience' for women: a) to obey her parents when young, b) to obey her husband when married, and c) to obey her children when old. It may be natural for a girl to obey her parents when she is young, but in what way is she to obey her husband after marriage?'[6] The book further stated that 'even if the husband is a drunkard or is addicted to sensual pleasures, or abuses and scolds her, and thus goes to the extreme of dissipation and lechery, the wife must still be obedient. She must respect her dissolute husband like heaven, and only protest to him with kind words and soft countenance.'[7]

---

[1] Fukuzawa, **Women**, 10
[2] Fukuzawa, **Women**, 12
[3] Fukuzawa, **Women**, 26
[4] Fukuzawa, **Women**, 75
[5] Fukuzawa, **Women**, 39
[6] Fukuzawa, **Learning**, 52
[7] Fukuzawa, **Learning**, 52

He was particularly outraged by the last chapter of **The Greater Learning of Women** whose 'attack on women is so severe that it may as well be called a spiteful work of literature full of curses and abuses heaped on women. The author pronounces that most women, seven or eight out of ten, have the five faults of women - indocility and disobedience, discontent and spitefulness, slander, jealousy, and shallow intellect - and, therefore, women are inferior to men.'[1] Yet it was not just neo-Confucianist texts which were to blame. Similarly 'A Buddhist scripture says that 'Women are full of sins'. Indeed, from this point of view, women are from birth no other than criminals who have committed great crimes.'[2] He gave a number of examples of 'harm done to women and children through the concept of the moral subordination of inferiors to superiors...'[3]

Fukuzawa was not content merely to diagnose some possible pressures on women, but went on to examine each part of the sexual and marital relationship and to advocate changes which would bring Japanese women closer to their emancipated western counterparts.

Starting with childhood and adolescence, he noted that 'The family customs are usually Confucian, which dictates that boys and girls after reaching the age of seven must not be seen together or share anything together.'[4] Consequently all relations between the sexes were discouraged before marriage. Speaking of the relations between young men and women, he suggested that 'there is practically none at all. If by chance there is such contact between the sexes, it is looked on with suspicion and it certainly will become a target of reprimand from elders.'[5] Consequently there was no chance for the prolonged courtship which was a necessary prelude for companionate marriage in the West. 'When they grow up to be of marriageable age, the rules of social oppression dictate that it is necessary to separate them further and further. Even to exchange words out of necessity is forbidden to them and the suspecting gazes around them make them hesitate. A glimpse of one another from a distance makes them uncomfortable. The result is their complete separation into entirely different worlds.'[6]

One consequence is that the marriage has to be arranged by others. 'Being brought up in such a restricted environment, when the time comes for the boy to marry, he does not know any girls. He will have to depend on the go-between's recommendation and meet a girl for the first time. This is called **miai**, a trial meeting.[7] All that happens at this 'trial meeting' is that 'the boy and girl manage to steal a glance at each other once, and they are married soon after.'[8] This is very different from the courtship which is essential for forming an equal relationship in the West, for '...according to the Western custom the man and the woman should look for and choose each other on their own, get to know each

---

[1] Fukuzawa, **Women**, 211
[2] Fukuzawa, **Learning**, 52
[3] Fukuzawa, **Learning**, 69
[4] Fukuzawa, **Women**, 128
[5] Fukuzawa, **Women**, 103
[6] Fukuzawa, **Women**, 118
[7] Fukuzawa, **Women**, 128-9
[8] Fukuzawa, **Women**, 129

other, and when they have made up their minds to marry, tell their parents, and, with their consent, hold a marriage ceremony.'[1]

Despite this difference, Fukuzawa did notice that Japanese children did seem to have more power than in many 'arranged marriage' societies. He noted that 'On the surface, it will appear as if marriages are arranged by the parents and the young folks only accept the final decision, but the truth is not so. The parents are only the ones to suggest and not the ones to decide.'[2] He elaborates what happens as follows. 'When the suggestion is made to the young people and if they are not happy with it, the issue cannot be forced. In such a case, the parents abandon their first choice and begin anew on a second search. Foreigners think that the Japanese marriage is arranged by the parents, but this is a false image constructed by ignorant people.'[3] In this one respect, the situation is not as bad as it might be. 'Therefore, aside from extreme cases, women today in general should not have much to complain about in the actual marriage process.'[4]

Although not at the extreme of arranged marriage, the lack of courtship, and other pressures, meant that there was little companionship in most Japanese marriages, Fukuzawa thought. He noted that 'Even after marriage, it is rare that the woman knows anything about her husband's reputation in society or how his colleagues regard him or what his accomplishments are.'[5] Thus, 'For ordinary people, when the husband comes home tired after a day's work, his wife is entirely insensitive to his labours, and she cannot offer proper concern when they talk together.'[6] The woman's main role, and the main purpose of the marriage is not companionship but procreation. 'In our society, the most humiliating expression for women is that a man's purpose in taking a wife is to ensure his posterity. The tone of this expression resembles 'The purpose of buying a rice cooker is to cook rice.'"[7] Again the kinship system biases the system against the woman. 'From this attitude stems the saying so often heard that the womb is a 'borrowed' thing. The meaning of this saying is that a child which is born into this world is its father's child and not its mother's - the rice that grew this year is born from the seed that was sown last year and the soil has no relation to it.'[8]

A particular way in which any companionship of husband and wife was stifled was through the pressure of the husband's parents. Ideally the eldest son, at least, would live with his parents and his strongest tie would be to them and particularly his mother. The new wife would compete with her mother-in-law and traditionally came a poor second. Fukuzawa rightly gives a good deal of attention to this important structural tension in the Japanese family.

He noted the inhibiting effects of the parents. While 'The in-laws who live with the couple...will pray for the happy relations between their son and his wife...at the same time they pray that the couple will not become too intimate. If a tender

---

[1] Fukuzawa, **Women**, 226
[2] Fukuzawa, **Women**, 226
[3] Fukuzawa, **Women**, 226
[4] Fukuzawa, **Women**, 227
[5] Fukuzawa, **Women**, 129
[6] Fukuzawa, **Women**, 130
[7] Fukuzawa, **Women**, 48
[8] Fukuzawa, **Women**, 48-9

sentiment seems to appear between them, the older folks become alarmed.'[1] As just one example, he noted that 'when the husband sets off on a long journey and the wife shows emotion at the parting or when the wife is ill and the husband tries to nurse her, the parents-in-law regard it as unsightly and warn them against it.'[2] The pressures against any show of affection extended outwards to the neighbours as well. Thus when husband and wife set off for a journey 'the present practice for them is to walk apart for a while and when they reach a predesignated spot, they meet and begin to walk side by side. The reason for this devious device is that they have many acquaintances around their house and it is embarrassing for the couple to be seen together.'[3] Yet the greatest pressure was always the co-resident, or nearby presence, of the parents in law.

Fukuzawa realized that this was a structural contradiction, not a matter of individual personalities. 'The mothers-in-law are not all wicked women, nor are the new wives. Without regard to being good or bad in character, the relations between the two are almost always at odds. The reason cannot be in the characters of the parties; it must be in the general atmosphere.'[4] Almost always there was a huge tension. 'Only one out of a hundred households made up of several young and old couples living together under the same roof will truly preserve peace and harmony among them. I do not exaggerate in saying that the remaining ninety-nine are what you would call paradise outside and purgatory inside with inmates made up of fake saints and false noble wives.'[5] At other times he put the odds against a harmonious mother and daughter-in-law relationship much higher. 'Thus, the relations between in-laws, regardless of the characters of each member of the household, will not be like that of true parents and child, except for a very rare case of one in a thousand or even ten thousand.'[6]

There was only one solution, which was for the generations to live entirely separately, as in the West. He noted that 'There are some families in which the newly married couple live apart from the parents. This I consider a very wise step, most appropriate to human nature.'[7] He believed that 'the ideal way is to have the young couple, as soon as they are married, settle in a new home of their own apart from their parents.'[8] Indeed it was not just a matter of living apart, but of having as little to do with each other as possible. 'In short, it is important to let the two families have as few points of contact as possible.'[9]

Fukuzawa also believed that the subordination of women was both reflected in and caused by other institutions. One of these was the plurality of marital and sexual relations in Japan. He noted that 'The West is made up of countries, in all of which monogamy - one wife to one husband - is the law, while Japan is a country where one husband may have many wives simultaneously. Could there

---

[1] Fukuzawa, **Women**, 120
[2] Fukuzawa, **Women**, 120
[3] Fukuzawa, **Women**, 120
[4] Fukuzawa, **Women**, 229
[5] Fukuzawa, **Women**, 123
[6] Fukuzawa, **Women**, 229
[7] Fukuzawa, **Women**, 188
[8] Fukuzawa, **Women**, 230
[9] Fukuzawa, **Women**, 230

be any contrast greater and more serious than this?'[1] He noted that 'A man of high rank and of wealth had many concubines, with the result that both the wife and the concubines suffered from small shares in the man's attention. This is a well-known fact.'[2] On the other hand, middling and poorer people resorted to prostitutes. Nor, given the lack of emotion within marriage and the tensions with the in-law relations, could he blame them. 'When one realizes that men are cut off entirely from establishing normal and friendly associations with women, and that they are confined to dull and lifeless relationships, it becomes natural that once they evade the restrictions, they will seek the extremes of freedom, or licentiousness...'[3] Whereas in the West, the home was the place to relax and to feel warmth, often in Japan it was necessary to escape from it. 'The fact is that the houses of concubines and the gay quarters are a separate world free from social rules and customs, the only havens where one may escape from social oppression.'[4] All of this was a very old and understandable pattern in Japan, but it must be changed. 'It is true that this Japanese practice of polygamy has a history of some unknown thousands of years. But now that the whole country has advanced into the modern civilization, I had thought that some scholars would turn their attention to this question and endeavour to devise some corrective measures.'[5]

The structural tensions in the family and the very weak position of women was also reflected in the ending of marriage. 'Divorce, which is very common and frequent in this country, must be caused by many factors, but the most important one is the non-existence of social intercourse between men and women.'[6] There were seven grounds for divorce, according to neo-Confucian thought, the first two which Fukuzawa gave are particularly revealing. 'i) A woman shall be divorced for disobedience to her father-in-law or mother-in-law. ii) A woman shall be divorced if she fail to bear children, the reason for this rule being that women are sought in marriage for the purpose of giving men posterity.'[7] The latter, Fukuzawa commented 'indeed is a preposterous statement without reason or human sentiment behind it.'[8] If the husband died, the widow was left in a very difficult position for there was a great deal of pressure against re-marriage. 'My consistent advice for such a person has been remarriage, but Japanese society is still very unreceptive to such a concept, and even among educated people, there are very few who support it. The general attitude is to recognize widowhood as a beautiful virtue in a woman. Some even say this is an extension of the saying about a virtuous woman never taking two husbands. It is sad to see such advocates placing obstacles in the way of remarriage.'[9]

Fukuzawa's extensive writing on women and family relations partly reflected his desire to introduce selected aspects of the marriage pattern which he had seen and read about in the West to Japan, in particular monogamy. Yet he also

---

[1] Fukazawa, **Women**, 139
[2] Fukuzawa, **Women**, 19
[3] Fukuzawa, **Women**, 124
[4] Fukuzawa, **Women**, 124
[5] Fukuzawa, **Women**, 139
[6] Fukuzawa, **Women**, 128
[7] Fukuzawa, **Women**, 179-80
[8] Fukuzawa, **Women**, 181
[9] Fukuzawa, **Women**, 239-40

wanted to change the emphasis on various features of the western system. We can see this when he wrote that 'the relation between husband and wife should not depend on love alone. Besides love and intimacy, there should be an element of mutual respect.'[1] Mutual support, intimacy and sharing was the perfect form. 'The true meaning of marriage should be for a husband and a wife to share a house, helping and being helped, enjoying the greatest happiness in life.'[2]

Thus the pattern that he advocated was neither the 'traditional' Japanese one, nor the western. Toshiko Nakamura compared his treatment of marriage and the family with my own model of the English marriage system and found significant differences. In England, romantic love was the ideal basis for marriage. Fukuzawa, however, 'expected the feelings based on morality between men and women rather than romantic love' to be the basis of marriage, that is to say 'Respect'. 'Love and Affection' were specifically confined to the parent-child relationship. Secondly, while Christianity and directly religious symbolism and ritual was a central context of western marriage, religion, as such, was much less important in Japanese marriage. Finally, the western family system was based on strong individualism. Apart from husband and wife, all relationships were based on contracts or rules. In Japan the whole family of parents and children was a moral zone, based on mutual respect and affection and excluding contract. Contractual relations started outside the nuclear family.[3]

Fukuzawa also had a wider aim, for he realized that the inequality of the genders was both a cause and consequence of the wider inequalities which ran through Japanese society. What he really objected to was the link between political and family relations which was explicit in neo-Confucian thought. Above all, Fukuzawa attacked the Confucian assumption of a direct parallel between all the five relations, the ruler-ruled, husband-wife, parent-child, brother-brother, master-servant. He attacked the assertion that the family was a mirror of the polity, and hence any objection to male or parental power was also treason, and he attacked on the other side the assertion that the state relations mirrored the family, and hence to attack a superior was also unfilial, impious, unnatural. On the latter he argued that 'if we consider the facts more deeply, the relation between government and people is not that of flesh and blood. It is in essence an association of strangers.'[4] If this were so, then 'Personal feelings cannot be the guiding principle in an association between strangers. It is necessarily based on the creation of a social contract.'[5] In other words, he was driving a wedge between kinship and politics.

This was truly revolutionary. Most absolutist states, whether China or Louis XIV's France, tried to combine these. Filmer in seventeenth century England in his **Patriarcha** had tried to do the same. But Fukuzawa echoes John Locke almost word for word in arguing that only mutual affection and mutual contract could be the basis for both the relations in the State and the Family. Blind obedience, uncritical submissiveness were wrong whether in the State or the

---

[1] Fukuzawa, **Women**, 33
[2] Fukuzawa, **Women**, 48
[3] Nakamura, 'Fukuzawa'.
[4] Fukuzawa, **Learning**, 70-1
[5] Fukuzawa, **Learning**, 71

Family. All people, including women, had natural and inalienable rights. This was an enormous change, but Fukuzawa was confident that it was happening. 'Recently we Japanese have undergone a great transformation. The theory of human rights has flooded the land and has been universally accepted.'[1]

He realized that the implications of changing one part of the social system, gender relations, would change everything. 'People may say that the foregoing argument is all logical, but from a practical point of view, the extension of women's rights today means disturbing the social order and it cannot be approved without reservation. However, it is inevitable that rectifying social evils will entail some readjustments. If one wants to avoid that disturbance, one will have to sit in silence and forbearance.'[2] And indeed, he showed in his own life the immense difficulties of changing the whole family system in one generation. In relation to his own family he found himself caught in contradictions. He noted the difficulty in his **Autobiography**. 'Some moralists are advocating love for all men in the whole world. I would be a beast not to give my own children equal love and privilege. However, I have to remember the position of my eldest son who will take my place and become the centre of the family after my death. So I must give him some privileges.'[3] This was privileging the oldest child. He made less explicit his failure to live up to his preaching on the equal education of women. While he wrote that 'Among my family of nine children, we make no distinction at all in affection and position between boys and girls'[4], this is not how one daughter remembers her childhood.

Carmen Blacker describes the following 'personal communication' from Mrs Shidachi, Fukuzawa's only surviving daughter, whose testimony shows that 'Fukuzawa failed entirely to put his precepts into practice in the upbringing of his own daughters.' He left their education entirely to the mother who was 'very conservative' and convinced of the innate inferiority of women.' Consequently 'Mrs Shidachi was never allowed out alone, never allowed to express her opinion in the presence of her elders, and never allowed to speak to guests when they came to the house...she was allowed next to no contact with men until her marriage at the age of eighteen, and even then her opinion was not consulted. Her education was, in fact, very little different from other girls 'except in so far as she learned English.'[5] A slightly different interpretation is given by Keiko Fujiwara who describes Fukuzawa's various attempts to educate his daughters, trying schools and then private tutors and commenting that 'Perhaps he was disappointed in school education, for he never did send his two youngest daughters to school. They were taught entirely by tutors at home. In these irregular attempts to educate his daughters, we can see the figure of a father struggling to provide the best education for his daughters.'[6]

This is a reminder that there is a considerable gap between the autobiographical reminiscences of Fukuzawa, dictated in his mid-sixties year, and his actual behaviour. Just as Craig shows that he selectively re-arranged his

---

[1] Fukuzawa, **Civilization**, 182; Fukuzawa was speaking of the early 1870's.
[2] Fukuzawa, **Women**, 195
[3] Fukuzawa, **Autobiography**, 300
[4] Fukuzawa, **Autobiography**, 299
[5] Blacker, **Fukuzawa**, 157-8
[6] Fukuzawa, **Women**, xiv

political activities in the **Autobiography** to present himself as detached and a-political[1], so his self-portrait needs to be treated with caution as an indication of his actual behaviour in other respects.

Yet rather than taking this gap between precept and practice as an indication of hypocrisy or weakness, it is better to see it as evidence of one of the many enormously strong pressures upon Fukuzawa. He tried to change almost everything in Japan, the political, economic, legal, moral, technological and social systems. All this was to be effected within twenty or thirty years in an old and complex civilization. It is hardly surprising that not everything was achieved and much has, in fact, remained unchanged below the surface. For our purposes here, what is interesting is to see how he perceived the essence of western family systems and their difference from the Japanese tradition.

---

[1] Craig, 'Fukuzawa', 103, n.7

13. THE ACHIEVEMENT AND THE LEGACY

In terms of his life and experiences Fukuzawa embodied great contradictions. He moved in one lifetime from one type of world into its almost complete opposite. Furthermore this forced upon him deeper and wider comparisons than any of them. Although he spent less effort on working out a sophisticated methodology than his European counterparts, he concentrated with intense concern on the riddle of the nature of the modern world, and how it could be achieved in Japan.

We shall see that his picture was very much like that of his western counterparts. Equality, individualism, liberty and the separation of spheres were the essential underpinnings for wealth and technological success. But there were other things which they took for granted but which he specified, for example the art of public speaking and discussion, confrontational politics, the relative equality of men and women, individual rights and modern accounting. All these Fukuzawa had to explain and teach to his fellow countrymen. But in essence, for most of his life, he proclaimed the Enlightenment message; wealth and power would follow a rise in equality, liberty and individualism. Technological imports without these changes would be worthless.

What makes Fukuzawa special is that his message coincided with the Meiji Restoration when his ideas suddenly became absorbed into the official policy of Japan. A relatively backward society, caught in many of the traps of the agrarian world - hierarchy, a certain degree of absolutism, technological stagnation - suddenly attempted to 'join the west'. No other Asian country had every attempted to do this, let alone succeeded in making the massive transformation in just two generations.

The amazing fact is that, partly on the basis of the blueprint, a simplified replica of the best of the Enlightenment, Japan performed the miracle, effected the exit from the agrarian world. Within fifty years it had developed from an isolated and relatively weak Asian polity into one of the great world powers which had defeated China and Russia. The growth of its industrial production, of its exports and of its agriculture was astounding. It had found the secret bridge from the agrarian world. The importation of western science and technology, though an essential part of this transformation, was only a part. The cultural, social and political changes were equally important. The fact that the same technology and science were available to China, South-East Asia and India, yet had little dramatic effect there for some eighty years after the Japanese transformation, shows how much more was involved.

Of course there were many other necessary pre-conditions in Japan; the craft skills, ingenuity, hard work, self-discipline, co-operativeness and flexibility of the work force. Yet all of these had been present for two hundred and fifty years of peace and increasingly easy taxation and had led nowhere in particular. It could be argued that it was the opening of Japan, and particularly the adoption of the Enlightenment message which tipped the balance from internal predation to internal production. Fukuzawa added little to the theoretical subtlety of the earlier analysis, but he was a highly intelligent thinker who sought to relay its central message, an enormously energetic man who sought to propagate these new views as widely as possible, and a man who was lucky enough to find that the tide was flowing with him.

Thus the miracle of the exit from agraria had been reproduced in a civilization what was in many respects different from its earlier home. Fukuzawa was in the end wiser than Marx, whose blueprint, with its closure of the separations between spheres by merging ideology and polity, taking equality far beyond its productive bounds, and creating the greatest despotisms the world has ever known, was a disaster. That a modern system of industry with some of its underpinning happened in Japan some two generations earlier than anywhere else in Asia is not unconnected to the work of Japan's greatest modernizer and analyst of modernity, Yukichi Fukuzawa. He deserves his place on the highest denomination Japanese bank-note.

*

One keen insight into the importance of non kin-based associationalism is given by Fukuzawa, who saw it from the outside. He had experienced in his childhood a world dominated by the institutional rigidities of hierarchy and the conformities of holistic familism. He had started to escape from this in Japan by moving from his home town into the great cities of Osaka and Tokyo. Yet in neither of these, beyond the glimpses in Ogata's school and elsewhere, could he see how a new institutional order could be constructed. This is what fascinated him on his visits to the West and particularly England where he was intrigued by various types of association.

So when Fukuzawa returned to Japan he tried to build up both the institutions and the arts of associationalism, that 'civil society' which alone could provide the foundational structure for modernity. There were the social and political clubs of the West, so he founded the Kojunsha social club in Tokyo, which survives to this day. It was specifically designed to emulate the London clubs, to foster discussion and a mature approach to politics, a place to talk and create networks of trust and information, share warmth and solidarity. Another kind of association, for the pursuit of knowledge, is the university, an archetype in the West of fellowship and equality. The university had been crucial in the development of western arts and science, yet it had never developed in China and Japan. So Fukuzawa started a high school which later developed into the first private Japanese university, Keio.

Or again there were the exchange banks of the West, without which Japan was losing much of its wealth. So he helped to set up one of the first new-style banks. Likewise he was active in the effort to form a modern police force and founded one of the first daily newspapers. Yet the institutions of association were not enough. He needed to go further, for without the skills to use the institutions they would never work. Practices which had long been taken for granted in the West, the arts of structured conversation, the art of the conference or public meeting, the art of making and listening to speeches (and even of clapping), the art of argument and methods of proof, the art of keeping the accounts of associations in order, all these basic skills had to be learnt for they existed, if at all, only in rudimentary form in Japan before the 1870's.

So Fukuzawa wrote a book on the art of public speaking and built a 'speech hall' in which to practice it. He wrote about the art of argument. He wrote a manual to introduce double-entry book keeping. And in all his writing and public speaking he kept his style simple and accessible so that real communication could take place. Through this and his best-selling descriptions of Western institutions, including the numerous techniques of civil society, he helped to undermine the older, rigid order and replace it with a more open, pluralistic and associational one. Thus he showed both an appreciation of the secret of Western civilization, the separation of spheres, and a deep understanding of the organizational technology of civil society which makes such a separation possible. He learnt from England, Holland and America the ways in which to open up a society, to build up those counter-veiling institutions, those 'secondary powers' which Montesquieu and Tocqueville and Maitland realized were essential for the pursuit of liberty, equality and wealth. This is why he is a principal architect of a modern, free, equal and wealthy Japan.

BIBLIOGRAPHY

The bibliography includes all works referred to in the text, except for those by Fukuzawa. His work is listed at the front of the work. All books are published in London, unless otherwise indicated.

The following abbreviations have been used.

>ed. edited or editor
>edn edition
>eds. editors
>Jnl. Journal
>n.d. no date
>tr. translated by
>Univ. University

Blacker, Carmen, 'The First Japanese Mission to England', *History Today*, vii (Dec.1957).

Blacker, Carmen, *The Japanese Enlightenment, A Study of the Writings of Fukuzawa Yukichi*, Cambridge, 1969.

Chamberlain, Basil Hall, *Japanese Things, Being Notes on Various Subjects Connected with Japan* (1904),

Tokyo, 1990.

Craig, Albert M., 'Fukuzawa Yukichi: The Philosophical Foundations of Meiji Nationalism' in Robert E. Ward (ed), *Political Development in Modern Japan*, New Jersey, 1968.

Griffis, W.E., *The Mikado's Empire*, 2 vols., New York, 1903.

Jansen, Marius B. (ed), *Cambridge History of Japan; the Nineteenth Century*, vol.v, Cambridge, 1989.

Kato, Shuichi, *A History of Japanese Literature*, Vol.3, The Modern Years, tr. Don Sanderson, *Tokyo*, 1979.

Kodansha *Encyclopedia of Japan*, Tokyo, 1983.

Kodansha, Japan. *An Illustrated Encyclopedia*, Tokyo, 1993.

Koestler, Arthur, *The Lotus & the Robot*, 1960

Macfarlane, Alan, *The Savage Wars of Peace: England, Japan and the Malthusian Trap*, Oxford, 1997

Macfarlane, Alan, *The Riddle of the Modern World; liberty, wealth and equality*, 2000.

Nakamura, Toshiko, 'Fukuzawa Yukichi's Ideas on Family in Civilization', parts. 1-3, *Hokkaido Law Review*. vol. XLIV, Nos. 3,4,6 (1993).

Nishikawa, Shunsaku, 'Yukichi Fukuzawa (1835-1901)', in *Prospects*, vol.XXI, no.2, UNESCO, 1991, reprinted in Fukuzawa Yukichi nenkan, vol.20, Dec. 1993.

Popper, Karl, *The Open Society and Its Enemies*, 1966.

Sugiyama, Chuhei, 'Fukuzawa Yukichi', Enlightenment and Beyond; Political Economy Comes to Japan, eds. Chuhei Sugiyama and Hiroshi Mizuta, Tokyo, 1988.

Yasukawa, Jyunosuke, 'Fukuzawa Yukichi', in *Ten Great Educators of Modern Japan*, ed. Benjamin C. Duke, Tokyo, 1989.

APPENDIX

Yukichi Fukuzawa's Ideas on the Family and the History of Civilization

By Professor Toshiko Nakamura, Hokkai-Gakuen University, Japan

1. Historical background

Yukichi Fukuzawa(1835-1901) is one of the greatest men of Japan. He is usually thought to have committed himself to westernize Japan in almost every social field, which included the subject of women and family. But his argument about women and family is very rich and related to his ideas about man and society in civilization. In this article, I would like to show his theory on the history of civilization and how he thought about man and society, which relates to his ideas on family and women.

Fukuzawa was born in 1835, when the Tokugawa government ruled Japan. The Tokugawa era lasted from 1603 to 1868. Its regime was based on the feudal system. Japan was divided into many local districts governed by samurai lords. At the top, there was the Shogun who was the top samurai lord. Social relations were based on hierarchy. Samurai was the top, then peasant, artisan and merchant. The Tokugawa government adopted Confucianism as the official ideology because it was thought to be the idea which justified the social hierarchy.

Fukuzawa's family belonged to the lower samurai class. His father was dead when he was three. The children of a samurai family usually started learning Chinese classics (including Confucian text books) from around seven, but he could not do so until fourteen. However, he especially liked books on history and mastered them very well. So we will see the influence of the Confucian classics in the later stage of his life.

The Tokugawa government took the policy of national seclusion from the mid seventeenth century for more than 200 years. But in 1853, Commodore Perry with his U.S. squadron came to Japan and demanded the country be opened. The Japanese Tokugawa government descended into confusion, and social hierarchy was shaken. Many men of the samurai class started to think about changing Japan. Fukuzawa was one of them. Some people thought it would be better to go back to the ancient way, and others thought it would be good to modernize Japan like the western countries. Fukuzawa hated the hierarchical social system and Confucianism as Tokugawa ideology. So he started to learn Dutch, because at that time Netherlands was the only western country allowed to trade with Japan, while English became widespread after Japan opened the country. He went to U.S.A. twice and Europe once as a member of the mission of Tokugawa government, and brought back many western books which he was going to translate into Japanese.

Japanese political turmoil ended with regime change in 1868. The Shogun (the highest samurai lord) returned his power to the emperor, which was called the Meiji restoration. So Fukuzawa lived his life in two different societies. The first half in feudal, and the second half modern. After Meiji restoration he tried to make Japan a liberal and democratic country. Most leaders of the samurai class became ministers of Meiji government, but Fukuzawa remained to be independent and tried hard to modernize Japan. He founded a university, set up a publisher, a newspaper, and helped to set up an insurance company, he taught about the commercial and political activities of the west and tried to practice them. So he had a great influence in every social field in Japan. Also, he wrote a lot about women's rights and family relations which was (and still is) exceptional as a leading man. As his ideas on family and women is very much related to his argument on the history of civilization, I have to start from his ideas on civilization.

2. Fukuzawa's ideas on civilization

The history of civilization

Though Fukuzawa wrote a lot of articles during his life time, most important among them is 'An Outline of a Theory of Civilization'. In 1874 he decided to stop translating western books and concentrated on studying the theory of civilization. He read the books of western scholars such as Guizot, Buckle and J. S. Mill and wrote some plans and drafts. He discussed them with friends and students before publishing the work in 1875. So we can see that he tried very hard to write this book.

In 'An Outline', he wrote about the history of civilization which human societies would go through as they developed. He divided the history into three stages, which were 'savage ', 'half civilized', and 'civilized'. Every society must go along the path until they reach the final stage of civilization. Surely he adopted this idea from western books he had read.

Then what does Fukuzawa think are the elements which make the development of civilization possible? He thinks there must be two elements. One is the advancement of 'intellectual ability (chi)' and 'virtue (toku)' of man which enables him to get material comfort in life and have dignity as a human. Another is the improvement of 'human social relations (jinnkan-kousai)'. Together they make our society develop towards the final stage of civilization. Then how is it possible? His explanation is as follows.

In the savage stage, people have no 'intellectual abilities' to understand the rules of nature. So they don't know how to deal with nature or control it. If they experience a natural calamity or good fortune, they tend to think that some evil or good Kami (god) which is beyond their control is the cause. The same can be said about their social relations. In this stage of civilization, there must be oppressive rules in society. But people never understand the reason or background of the oppressive rules. They only fear the oppressions thinking they are just like natural calamities. They have no 'intellectual abilities' to understand them and oppose them. Everything is decided by the ruler's orders. So is their moral code. People are forced to obey the ideological moral code ordered by the ruler.

The process of civilization begins when 'the intellectual ability' of man develops first. Then man starts to doubt everything around him. He wants to know the reason or the cause of natural calamities and tries to avoid them by doing something. So he can control nature by his 'intellectual ability'. What comes next?

He also starts to doubt and think about the situation of his own being too. He doubts the Confucian ideological teachings and the stories of loyal Samurai which tell him how to behave. He starts thinking by his own reason what kind of person he should be. So he 'gets his freedom of spirit, why not his freedom of body'. In other words he gets control of himself and becomes independent. He decides what kind of person he wants to be and what and how to manage to do on his own. His moral code is decided by himself **from within**, not by the ruler's orders **from outside** himself. Fukuzawa thought if man got autonomy and had his own moral code by himself, man could be called 'virtuous'. Fukuzawa named such a kind of moral code 'private virtue', because it related only to man's own being. He thought it important, because if man was independent, he must not rely on anything but himself especially in relation to what kind of person he was to be.

Once man becomes independent and gains autonomy, then he starts to think about his social relations. Now he is able to use his 'intellectual ability' and knows what kind of person he wants to be. Then he thinks and decides by his own reason what and how to deal with other people. He knows what is wrong and what is right to do to other people. So he must be virtuous in social relations. Fukuzawa called this kind of moral code 'public virtue'. If man becomes virtuous and behaves accordingly, the human relation around him would be improved. This is the second element of the development of civilization.

The more man gets his 'intellectual ability' and becomes able to decide his moral code not by ideology **from outside** but **from within** himself, the more he will be able to behave 'virtuously' towards other people. This process improves the social relations around him.

Fukuzawa imagined that the social relations of man could be drawn as concentric circles. The first circle of social relation is family and it should be improved first. Then next would be the relations in the nation. People go through this process one by one and civilization develops until it reaches the highest stage of civilization where everyone is intellectual as Newton and virtuous as Confucius. The whole world is in peace and like one family. So there will be no robbery or dispute, and people need not lock their doors or make contractual documents for proof. Fukuzawa called it 'the peaceful world of civilization (bunmei-no-taihei)'. But he knew it would be realized many thousands years away in the future.

The Confucian framework of civilization and society

As I already mentioned, Fukuzawa read a lot of western books and learned the theory of the history of civilization from them. We can see their influence on his argument about the historical process of civilization. We also know he tried hard to modernize Japan. So we tend to think that Fukuzawa tried to imitate western civilization abandoning the old ideas. But, if we read his argument carefully, we can see that he did not only absorb the ideas of western scholars but he tried to do so having his own framework of thinking about man and society. He learned Chinese classics when he was young and liked especially classics on history. He read them many times and mastered them very well. Though he attacked Confucian ideology in the Tokugawa feudal system in his articles, it was just the ideological function of Confucianism. His basic frame of thinking was Confucian. He understood the western theory of the history of civilization through the Confucian framework and thought they were compatible and fit together well.

It is well recognized when we see Fukuzawa's ideas of man. We saw that Fukuzawa insisted that man had to have a spirit of independence and autonomy to develop civilization. It meant man developed his 'intellectual ability' and 'virtue' and became independent. We may find similar ideas on man and society in western books. However, he always referred the man as a 'Head of ten thousand things (banbutsu-no-rei)' which was the basic Confucian idea of man. In Neo Confucian philosophy, man has a 'true nature' which must come out as he trains himself to be a virtuous man. Fukuzawa also thought man had a 'true heart (honshin)' as his core, and it could emerge only by working hard to develop his 'intellectual ability' and 'virtue'. (This is the background idea of his famous popular book, 'An Encouragement of Learning'). Fukuzawa's aim is not becoming good and virtuous as in the Confucian ideal but becoming a man of 'independence and self respect (dokuritsu-jison)'. This idea seems to coincide with the western idea of independent man. But we can find out a similar phrase already in the books of Confucian scholars in the Tokugawa period. So perhaps it was not Fukuzawa's original idea but there were such ideas among Confucian scholars in Tokugawa period. Fukuzawa expected people of the samurai class to become such a kind of men who would lead the process of civilization in Japan and he believed they could be so.

Fukuzawa also wrote that if a man became 'intellectual' and 'virtuous', i.e. the 'Head of ten thousand things', then the social relations around him would be improved. He thought this improvement proceeded from the inner to the outer concentric circles around man. So from family to nation and finally to the whole world. He wrote many times that only 'after man became independent, then his household would become independent, after that his nation would become independent and the whole world would be independent'. His famous phrase came from a Neo Confucian text book.

The theme of Confucian philosophy is how to become a virtuous man and govern the country by virtue. The way to do it through Neo-Confucian philosophy is as follows. First a man must know the reason (ri) of the world (ten) (kakubusu-chichi). Then he tries to follow reason from his heart and behave accordingly (seii-seishin). By doing so, he will govern himself and become a virtuous man (shushin). This process which made man virtuous was thought to be very important in Neo Confucian philosophy. Then he can administer his household (seika), and then govern his country (chikoku) and finally make peace in the whole world (heitenka).

We can understand Fukuzawa's explanation about the process of civilization well if we use this framework. In Neo Confucian ideas, the reason of the world which man must know meant the Chinese classical idea of the rule of the world based on yin-yan theory. But Fukuzawa changed this meaning to the rules of nature based on modern science. His idea of 'intellect' meant the ability to think in a rational way and he insisted that man must be 'intellectual' to understand and conquer nature. Then in the Confucian precept, man must try to behave himself in order to follow the reason of the world based on yin-yan theory. Fukuzawa changed this to mean that man must behave himself by following his reason and become 'virtuous'. Then he will be independent and govern himself (isshin-dokuritsu). After that, his social relation will improve and his household and his nation will be independent accordingly (ikka-dokuritsu, ikkoku-dokuritsu). So his idea of the history of civilization had the same structure with Neo Confucian ideas of man and the world. Perhaps Fukuzawa read and understood the western books about the history of civilization through this Neo Confucian framework of thinking in order to see the world and modernize it to include the knowledge of modern natural science.

Fukuzawa argued that as the history of civilization developed, it would reach the highest stage of civilization i.e. 'peaceful world of civilization'. The idea that history had a goal to reach was surely from the western books. But when we read his explanation about 'the peaceful world', we can see it very much looks like the descriptions of 'the world of everyone's peace (daido-no-yo)' in a Chinese classic book (raiki). In Confucian philosophy the ideal world was at the beginning of the history. But Fukuzawa put it at the end of history followed to the western ideas, maintaining the same description of the ideal world.

3. Family relation in the history of civilization

Man-woman relations

In the explanation of Fukuzawa's ideas on the history of civilization, I showed that he mentioned all the social relations including family relation as public and used the word 'private' only for himself (see his argument about 'private virtue and public virtue'). Also his argument about social relations started from family relations. Again, he described the ideal 'peaceful world of civilization' as a 'family'. So 'family' is a basic and important social relation in his idea of society. This is the characteristic of Fukuzawa's ideas of society which is very much different from the western social theory.

In Fukuzawa's ideas of society, family was the first sphere to be affected by the improvement of social relations in the history of civilization. He thought the relationship between man and woman was most basic and important because all the virtuous relations between people began here. He explained the man-woman relation would also change according to the development of civilization i.e. the development of 'intellectual ability' and 'virtue' of man. At the 'savage stage' where man (and of course woman) had no 'intellectual ability' or 'virtue', men and women wanted to have relationships with each other from natural instinct. Fukuzawa argued the feeling of 'love' at that stage was instinctive sexual passion just like animals. They felt love because their physical forms were different. So their relation would be mainly a physical one. He named it as 'physically communicated relation (niku-kou)'.

As history advances, man acquires his 'intellectual ability' and 'virtue', and becomes independent. Fukuzawa thought that the most important feature of this development relating to social relations was the ability to use language based on reason. So the development of 'intellectual ability' is the key to change the situation. Man and woman try to communicate with each other by language, not by direct physical action. Using language, they can get to know and understand each other's feelings very well. So, Fukuzawa called this type of relation a 'relation communicated by feeling (jou-kou)'. Then they love each other from their hearts. To know other's feeling is important because it means one can understand other's **inside**. As I mentioned in relation to the independence of man, Fukuzawa thought man's relationship with others must be **from the inside**, not forced **from the outside**. So the ideal relationship between people had to be from heart to heart.

Once people become able to understand each other, then a man must start to think about a woman as a 'Head of ten thousand things' like himself (or vice versa). He understands she is as independent as he. Then the way to show his 'love' is to 'respect' her and be gentle and kind to her (the same is said about woman). So their behaviour becomes very virtuous and they have mutual 'love and respect (kei-ai)' after all. 'Respect (kei)' is the very basic and important idea to become virtuous in Confucian philosophy. So we can see the influence of Confucianism here too in the relationship between man and woman. Fukuzawa thought even though man and woman understood and loved each other deeply, they were separate entities. Their relation was not like 'the better half' in the west. They could not act totally in the same way. So he emphasized the importance of 'jo' between man and woman which meant 'Do not do to others what you don't want to be done to you'. It looks just the same as western liberal thought. But he said he could find such an idea in old Confucian thought, and it was not necessary to introduce a new idea from the west.

Fukuzawa thought a woman was the same 'Head of ten thousand things' as man as far as she was 'intellectual' and 'virtuous'. The only difference between them was that they have different sexual organs. Other than that, they were completely the same, and there must be no difference or no different evaluation in their social activities. So almost a hundred years before modern feminism introduced the idea of 'gender' against 'sex' in 1970's, Fukuzawa had argued about the same kind of differentiation based on the Confucian idea of the 'Head of ten thousand things'. He even mentioned the possibility of 'free love' in 'the peaceful world of civilization'. (This idea may have come from 'the Modern Times movement' in America in the second half of the nineteenth century.) If man and woman develop their abilities as he thinks along with the civilization, their relation in 'the peaceful world' will depend totally on their free will and from the hearts. Then they set up their relations solely dependent on their 'love'. They are free to tie or dissolve their relations. But after mentioning these ideas, Fukuzawa reminded the readers that it was not yet the time to do that. The monogamous and lasting relation was the best choice at that time of civilization, he said.

Parent-child relations

This relation is different from the man-woman relation, because a child can never be equal to parent as a 'Head of ten thousand things' as his 'intellectual ability' is always underdeveloped in any stage of the history. Still the relation changes as history progresses. At the first savage stage, the parent loves his child as animals love their offspring. It is as it were animal love. But since parent is to be a 'Head of ten thousand things', his attitude must change as civilization develops. He starts to think about the child's welfare as he becomes intellectual himself and tries to help and guide his child and show the child the way to be a ' Head' (which means parent is 'virtuous' to his child). The child is always underdeveloped, so there must always be the imbalance of power between the parent and child. But if there is the imbalance of power between two people, the one who has power must try to fill the gap by using his power to help the disadvantaged one, not to oppress him.

This idea is just opposite to 'the preponderance of power (kenryoku-no-henchou)' of Confucian ideology in the Tokugawa regime which allowed people in power to use it to oppress the disadvantaged. Fukuzawa hated any kind of oppression. This is the reason why he attacked the Confucian ideology of the Tokugawa regime very fiercely. The Confucian ideology demanded there must be 'the preponderance of power' in every social relation (lord-vassal, man-woman, and parent-child etc.) and the lower person should always serve the upper person. Fukuzawa strongly opposed this idea and wanted people in power to become virtuous and use it to help the disadvantaged. (He categorized disadvantaged persons as 'the elderly, the infant, the small and the weak ').

The most important role of parent was to educate child to be a 'Head'. For Fukuzawa the educational role of adults was a kind of social duty for human beings. He always emphasized the influence of the parents' behaviour and insisted that parents must behave virtuously to show the good examples to children. These were the ideal family relations based on the development of civilization. He thought such kind of family relations existed at that time in Japan in some samurai class families. He took it as a model of the ideal relations in the state of civilization in his argument.

4. The meaning of 'An Outline of a Theory of Civilization'

Though Fukuzawa wrote about 'An Outline of a Theory of Civilization' rather optimistically as mentioned above, he clearly knew that the situation surrounding Japan was not so hopeful. At the beginning of the last chapter of 'An Outline', he wrote 'if you compare the civilization of the west and Japan, you must say that Japan is far behind the west. If there is a gap between them, naturally the forerunner will conquer the latecomer. So we must be vigilant and try to keep the independence of our nation.'

His analysis of the situation is as follows. The people of Japan are in a rather easy mood because they succeeded in the Meiji restoration and the following political changes went well. But, he warns, it is not the time to rest after finishing the political changes successfully. Japan has another problem. It is the relation with foreign countries. They deprive Japanese of their wealth by trade. Also they behave oppressively even though they permit equal rights for Japanese. Look at India. Look at China. So, the most important matter for Japan in the current situation is to keep independence. Independence means not merely the territory of the nation exists but people themselves protect their nation and keep their rights and dignity. So he declared to stand up to keep the independence of Japan. Even though he imagined 'the peaceful world of civilization', it was not the time to realize it. When every other nation competes to have the share of the world, Japan must also become eligible to compete with them or defend itself at least. He knew well that such nationalism was a bit narrow and biased from the view point of 'the peaceful world' but it was the reality at that time. So in the last part of 'An Outline' he wrote, 'Now, our goal is to keep the independence of our nation, and the civilization we aim **now** is the means to keep it.' In the last chapter he drew readers' attention many times to the fact that he was talking about the 'current situation' and commented that he used the word 'current' or 'now ' especially to think about problems of Japan **at that time**. So he warned people that they must not mix it up with the general theory of civilization.

So, in 'An Outline' Fukuzawa wrote about the general theory of civilization which was an ideal way to the goal, and in the last chapter the realistic analysis about the situation of Japan. He was not the kind of man who thought only the ideal theory or real politik. He always assessed the real situation along with the theory of ideal world. He explained his aim to write the book in the first two chapters of 'An Outline'. He emphasized the importance of deciding the aim of an argument and said his aim to write the book was to catch up with western civilization. So he mentioned about the general theory first, and then decided it was necessary to aim at the western civilization to keep the independence of Japan at that time.

By having these dual ways of the reality and the theory in mind, he could show two important points to Japanese people. One is that the gap between Japanese and western civilization did exist. However, another point is, Japan could catch up, because the gap was never very great on the long course of the history of civilization. If he did not think of the history of civilization which had the ideal world far beyond the western stage, it would have been difficult to believe that Japan could catch up with the west. The long history of civilization put the western civilization in a relative position, (it was not **the** civilization), and made people think the gap between Japan and the west was relatively small in the process of a long history. So this argument could have given a warning to Japanese people in one way, and encouraged them to catch up with the western civilization in another. Then what should Japanese people do to catch up with the west?

Fukuzawa thought that to copy the outer form of civilization was pretty easy. But he understood that the essence of western civilization was the independent spirit of people which he thought western people had, but was very difficult to create in Japan. However, there was some way to do it. It would be difficult if you think of creating it from nothing, but what if you use some things that already exist in Japan and change them? Fukuzawa thought it was possible. So in the end of 'An Outline', he wrote, 'moral ties of feudal system of the Tokugawa could be used as "the expedient means" of civilization to make man virtuous, if you understand the purpose of national independence correctly.' So he was determined to keep the independence of Japan and very flexible. He tried to use everything possible as 'expedient means' for the purpose. As I mentioned already, he expected the samurai class to become independent men and the samurai family was a kind of model of the family in civilization. He regarded people of samurai class as the candidates for leadership in the process of civilization in Japan, just like the middle class in England.

5. The different principles in family and nation

In his analysis of the history of civilization, Fukuzawa showed us that human relation improved from the nearest relationship. It means that from family relation to nation, and in the whole world. Man is the centre of the concentric circles of human relations and his social relation begins in the family sphere which is the nearest circle to man. Even though we set boundaries to divide each circle, they are not fixed. The boundaries will be blurred and fade away as the history of civilization progresses, because the social relations around man will improve from near to far over the boundaries of family and nation which we set to divide them now. He thought that Japanese civilization at that time had already developed as far as people had ideal relations in the family circle. So it was time to concentrate on the independence of the nation. It means that in the 'current' situation of civilization we have to have such boundaries of spheres as family and nation around us.

Fukuzawa thought there were different kinds of social relations based on different principles in different circles in society at that time. He explained that family relations were based on 'the sentimental bond (jou)' and 'virtue'. But relations in western society were based on rules, contracts, laws and international treaties 'now'. 'All of them are the means only to prevent bad behaviour. There is no spirit of virtue.' He was critical of such society but it was necessary to follow them to catch up. So he set off to lead Japan to catch up with western countries by modernizing Japanese society. Usually the family is not included in the 'social relation' in the west, but Fukuzawa included it and chose to keep it as it was based on different principle from the western social relations.

We know from historical studies that real family relations in the Tokugawa period was not so oppressive as had been thought judging by texts of Confucian teaching. We can see a lot of examples of intimate and caring relations inside families if we read diaries, letters and chronicles of that time. Women were independent and they went anywhere on their own. (Such a situation was very different from China, as many Chinese travellers noticed in their chronicles just after the Meiji restoration.) Man and woman had different roles, but they respected each other's role and helped each other. Wives had a strong power for management of the household and they could leave husbands when they wanted divorce. Fathers looked after their children more than today. (Of course, it was a part of the training of succession of their jobs.) Some fathers even took children to their working places when their mothers were ill. So perhaps Fukuzawa wrote his articles bearing such family relations in his mind. He thought it would be all right to leave family relations as they were and focused on the changes of social fields.

6. The problems of man-woman relation in the context of modernization

As we saw already, Fukuzawa thought the independence of the nation was most important at that time in Japan. So he devoted himself to modernizing Japan as a nation. As far as families were concerned, he thought it would be all right to leave them as they were. This was his analysis when he wrote 'An Outline' in 1875. But the real situation did not go as he had expected. In the 1880s the Meiji government turned its policy to be very conservative and tried to reintroduce the Confucian ideas as the basic ideology of their policy. So Fukuzawa was inevitably forced to fight against it, and wrote a few articles to oppose strongly the revival of Confucian ideology. It was rather a tricky and difficult task for him, because his strategy for civilization was to use every possible element of Tokugawa period as the expedient means to civilization. It might easily be mixed up with the conservative ideology of Confucianism. So he had to attack the Confucian ideology all the more fiercely. When we read his articles during this period we have to be very careful and think about these political situations.

This is also said about Fukuzawa's articles on family and women. He wrote them mainly from 1885 to 1888, when the revision of treaties with western countries which forced Japan in an unequal position was on the political table, and in 1899 just after the promulgation of the civil code of Japan. Those articles were written mainly to argue about the 'current' problems concerning man-woman relation in the context of modernization, with a fierce attack on Confucian ideology. Then what was the problem about men at that time?

It was the immoral behaviour of men. Fukuzawa argued that men started to behave immorally after the Meiji restoration. They were 'like horses freed without bits in the spring field'. In Tokugawa period the situation was different. Even though men were permitted to have concubines, it was under strict rules. But Fukuzawa said it had all changed. 'Nowadays men behave immorally without any restrictions. Men refuse to listen to their parents' opinion about marriage and even abandon their wives to marry with another'. Especially the leaders' behaviour was awful. They bought prostitutes without hesitation. Some even married them. This was not the way of behaviour of civilized people. He even said the Confucian moral code forced by Tokugawa government had been good to keep the moral behaviour of men.

Fukuzawa worried about the situation just because it might affect the revision of treaties. The western marriage system was monogamy. So what did western people think of Japan if they knew the situation? They would not recognize Japan as a civilized nation, which meant the revision of treaties would not be successful. Fukuzawa expected men to behave morally, or at least to hide immoral behaviour behind the scenes. He knew well even in western countries people did not always behave morally, but they tried to conceal those acts. So he advised Japanese men to do the same as western people. It might not be an ideal way but a necessary 'expedient way' to be a member of modern civilized nations.

Fukuzawa thought women were virtuous enough even by the standard of western civilization. Their problems would be some lack of social and political rights and responsibilities compared with western women. He advocated that women must be equally educated as men from the start, and they must have their own properties. He thought women would be able to carry their responsibilities by having those rights and exercising them. Fukuzawa mentioned that western women take the jobs in various fields, but it was a bit early to talk about it, he said. Japanese women had to change gradually with the change of their circumstances. So his articles were written to bring the social status of Japanese women up to the same level as western women. He expected Japanese women to take the role of management of their household as before in the mean time of modernization.

In 1894 Japan defeated China in the Sino-Japanese war. Fukuzawa was very delighted and perhaps relieved by the victory. It was a victory of Japanese civilization, because China once had been a great civilization but then half colonized by western countries.

Fukuzawa wrote his last major works on family and women in 1899. Japan succeeded in revision of the unequal treaties with the western countries by then and promulgated the Civil Code previous year. For Fukuzawa the promulgation of the Civil Code was 'a very great change', and 'the revolution of people's mind'. The newspaper he edited printed the articles of the Civil Code, and explained them to the readers. He might have thought that the equality between man and women has its solid ground in the Civil Code. Fukuzawa accepted it as the development of civilization. The time had come to be based on the concrete law, not the moral code by the ruler, to set up the relations between people as in western countries. That was his understanding. He was pleased that Japan had reached the same stage of civilization as western nations, which were based on rules, at the very last period of his life.

7. Conclusion

When we look back at our history, we know there have been many great changes in our society. The Meiji restoration is one of them. But people's life always continues despite those big changes of social structure. It would be impossible to change all the aspects of life, abandoning everything old. Fukuzawa knew this well or thought it was impossible and not necessary to do so. He applied a similar kind of attitude when he studied western social theories. He understood the western theory of history of civilization through the old

Confucian frame of thinking. He had the ideal way of civilization in mind and always assessed the reality of Japan in the context of the ideal civilization. He tried hard to find the way to apply the essence of western civilization, keeping the existing Japanese way of life. Fukuzawa went back and forth between these dual ways, and so he could be very realistic when necessary.

Even though western civilization was not the ideal way, Fukuzawa tried hard to catch up with the western civilization once he decided to keep Japanese independence. In Fukuzawa's thinking, Japanese family relations had to be kept being. But outside the family circle, i.e. in economic and political fields, Japan had to become as capitalistic and liberal as the west. Japanese people tried to imitate those social systems since Meiji without changing much of these close human relations. So we have always this double layer social structure. The outer structure of society is western, but the inner Japanese. We can see this double layers structure, in various combinations, in every aspect of social life in Japan. Perhaps this is what makes foreigners rather confusing when they try to understand Japanese people and society. But this was the way how Japan accepted western influences from outside.

Fukuzawa's ideas are as it were the mixture of three civilizations. Japanese, Chinese and western. They contain many suggestions which we who live in the westernized modern world have forgotten and can rediscover again. As far as the ideas on family is concerned, I can point out two important arguments. Firstly, we have alternative man-woman relation to the west. Fukuzawa showed us co-operative relation in which man and woman respected each other as independent individuals i.e. as the 'Head of thousand things' and was united by 'love and respect'. As Fukuzawa thought the family relation was the first **social** relation, people had to be independent and set up relations between individuals even in the family. It was different from the western idea of the 'better half' in which man and woman become one by 'romantic love'. The second important point is that his argument includes the relation with the disadvantaged. If we presuppose only an individual who is rational and independent, it would be difficult to think of society including the people who are not rational or independent. He thought the relation with the disadvantaged was different from the relation between independent individuals. This is also very suggestive for us to reconstruct the society including every kind of people who have some disadvantages.

Lastly and especially, we can see his struggle as an example of how to import the fruits of other civilization and apply them to the existing civilization. We are now living in the world of so called 'clash of civilizations'. So I think it is all the more important to know that there was a way to accept and implant the fruits of other civilizations and how it was done in Japan.

Bibliography

Yukichi Fukuzawa, *An Outline of a Theory of Civilization*, tr. David A. Dilworth and G. Cameron Hurst, Tokyo, 1973

Yukichi Fukuzawa, *Fukuzawa Yukichi on Japanese Women*, ed. Eiichi Kiyooka, Tokyo, 1988

Carmen Blacker, *The Japanese Enlightenment*, C.U.P., 1964

www.ingramcontent.com/pod-product-compliance
Lightning Source LLC
Chambersburg PA
CBHW080348170426
43194CB00014B/2721